BLUEPRINT

Science Key Stag

Teacher's Resource Book

Third Edition

Wendy and David Clemson

Stanley Thornes (Publishers) Ltd

First published in 1990 as Blueprints
Science 7-11 Teacher's Resource Book.
Second edition published in 1992.
Reprinted 1993 (twice), 1994 (twice)

Third edition published in 1995 by
Stanley Thornes (Publishers) Ltd
Ellenborough House
Wellington Street
CHELTENHAM GL50 1YW

98 99 00 / 10 9 8 7 6 5

A catalogue record for this book is available from the British Library.

ISBN 0–7487–2213–0

Typeset by Tech-Set, Gateshead, Tyne & Wear
Printed and bound in Great Britain by
Redwood Books, Trowbridge, Wiltshire

CONTENTS

Introduction	iv
How to Use This Book	vii
Topic Planner	viii
Blueprints Links	xii
Coverage of the Curriculum for Scotland and Northern Ireland	xiv
Common Requirements of the Programme of Study	1
Experimental and Investigative Science	15
Life Processes and Living Things	19
Materials and their Properties	50
Physical Processes	67
Record Sheets	107

INTRODUCTION

What is *Blueprints: Science?*
Blueprints: Science is a practical teacher's resource specifically written to fulfil all the requirements of the National Curriculum in science for primary schools. It is intended for all teachers, particularly non-science specialists, and provides comprehensive coverage in an easy-to-follow format. *Blueprints: Science* is a rich resource of practical ideas to use alongside other materials within your scheme of work. It gives children meaningful, relevant things to do. *Blueprints: Science Key Stage 1* provides activities for 5–7-year-olds. *Blueprints: Science Key Stage 2* includes activities for 7–11-year-olds. For each Key Stage there is a Teacher's Resource Book and a book of Pupils' Copymasters.

***Blueprints* and the National Curriculum**
This third edition of *Blueprints: Science* closely follows the revised publication *Science in the National Curriculum* (HMSO 1995). The Teacher's Resource Book is structured around the four main sections of the Programme of Study. The Pupils' Copymasters reinforce and extend the activities in this book and also provide materials for teacher-based assessment, for use alongside SATs.

***Blueprints* and topics**
Blueprints: Science is a flexible resource, and can be used in subject lessons devoted exclusively to the learning of science or in the learning of scientific principles while doing topic work. On pages viii–xi of this Teacher's Resource Book is a Topic Planner chart which lists many of the topics in common use. Alongside each topic title is an indicator to show in which Areas of Study there is work which can easily make a contribution to the topic.

Blueprints: Science Key Stage 2
This Teacher's Resource Book provides dozens of practical explorations and activities through Key Stage 2.

At the beginning of the book is the section of the Programme of Study which applies across all of the science curriculum – the 'common requirements'. Beneath each point in the Programme of Study are examples of activities drawn from the rest of the book, which could contribute to work relating to this section. Where appropriate, additional Areas of Study have also been included here.

The book is then arranged in four main sections. The sections relate to work which should be covered by children through this Key Stage. Within each section, the heading for work is a reproduced extract from the Statutory Provisions, comprising the title and applicable points from the Programme of Study.

Programme of study: Life processes and living things

Work on life processes should be related to pupils' knowledge of animals and plants in the local environment. Work on the variety of life in a habitat should be linked to the reasons for classifying living things.

1. Life processes
Pupils should be taught:
a that there are life processes, including nutrition, movement, growth and reproduction, common to animals, including humans;
b that there are life processes, including growth, nutrition and reproduction, common to plants.

In addition, at the front of each section, you will find a reproduction of the relevant Programme of Study, cross-referenced to the Areas of Study in this book and to Level Descriptions.

Materials and their properties

How the Areas of study in this book relate to the section of the Programme of study and Attainment target level descriptions. Programme of study		Areas of study and 'best fit' with Level descriptions: Level description 2	Level description 3	Level description 4	Level description 5
	Pupils should be taught: **e** about the water cycle and the part played by evaporation and condensation;			Area of study: 13	
	f that the changes that occur when most materials, *e.g. wood, wax, natural gas*, are burned are not reversible.			Area of study: 14	
3. Separating mixtures of materials	**a** that solid particles of different sizes, *e.g. those in soils*, can be separated by sieving;	Area of study: 15			
	b that some solids, *e.g. salt, sugar*, dissolve in water to give solutions but some, *e.g. sand, chalk*, do not;			Area of study: 16	
	c that insoluble solids can be separated from liquids by filtering;			Area of study: 16	Area of study: 17
	d that solids that have dissolved can be recovered by evaporating the liquid from the solution;				Area of study: 17
	e that there is a limit to the mass of solid that can dissolve in a given amount of water, and that this limit is different for different solids.				Area of study: 18

You will find a similar cross-reference on the Area of study heading, showing how its activities meet the Programme of Study, and a suggested 'best fit' with a Level Description.

Area of study 3 | P of S 1b | LD 2 | **SUSTAINING PLANT LIFE PROCESSES** C14

This cross-referencing means that you can easily identify parts of the Programme of Study being worked on, and have support in determining which Level Description best fits a child's work.

There are two record sheets at the back of the book, on which you can identify work you and the children have completed, and also note work done which has contributed to Experimental and Investigative Science.

The Pupils' Copymaster Book provides 97 photocopiable worksheets linked to many of the activities in this Teacher's Resource Book. The worksheets give the children a chance to record activities and results in an organised way, and in some cases to consolidate learning that has gone before. When completed, the worksheets can be added to the children's workfiles or used as exemplar material in pupil profiles. They may also be seen as a resource for teacher assessment. There are two record sheets at the back, on which you can note the copymasters that the children have made use of, and their experience of work contributing to:

- Experimental and Investigative Science
- Life processes and Living Things
- Materials and their Properties
- Physical Processes

Blueprints: Science Key Stage 2 provides coverage of all these sections of the Programme of Study for Levels 2–5. It is expected that most of the children should master Level 4, but Level 5 work is provided for those children who require work beyond Level 4.

Experimental and Investigative Science

This has been treated differently from the other areas of the science curriculum. It comprises half the science curriculum at Key Stage 2, and is about 'becoming a scientist', i.e. it concentrates on methods of scientific enquiry, rather than substantive knowledge. In the section for Experimental and Investigative Science there is a discussion of how the children can work to meet the requirements of the Programme of Study. We have, however, chosen to use activities in all the other parts of the book as vehicles for the acquisition of experimental and investigative skills. Symbols have been created to denote the coverage of these skills, and these are used throughout the rest of the book and in the copymasters to show how and where the experimental and investigative skills are being covered.

Experimental and investigative science skills symbols

Level 2

Turn ideas into investigations	Use apparatus	Observe and measure	Draw tables, charts and graphs	State whether results met predictions

Level 3

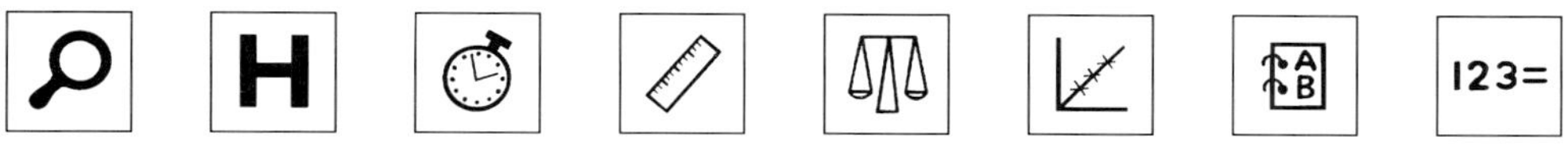

Turn ideas into investigations	Predict and hypothesise	Use apparatus	Observe and measure	Fair test	Draw tables, charts and graphs	Statements of data patterns	State whether results met predictions

Level 4

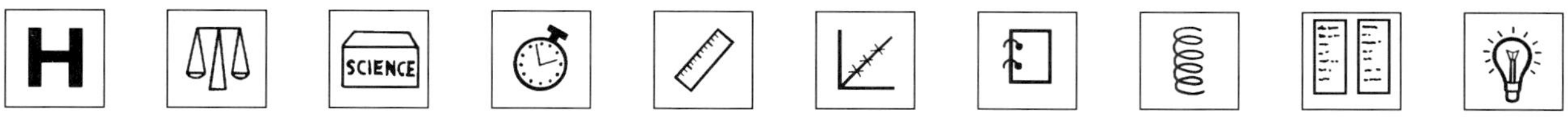

Predict and hypothesise	Fair test	Choose apparatus	Use apparatus	Observe and measure	Draw tables, charts and graphs	Prose description	Draw conclusions	State whether results met predictions	Explain conclusions

Level 5

Predict and hypothesise	Decide evidence to collect	Fair test	Choose apparatus	Use apparatus	Observe and measure	Check results by repeating

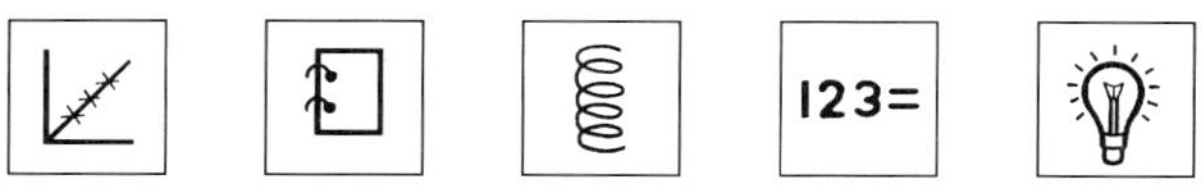

Draw tables, charts and graphs	Prose description	Draw conclusions	State whether results met predictions	Explain conclusions

A more detailed summary of how these skills are related to the Programme of Study and Attainment Target Level Descriptions is shown on pages 15–18.

Record keeping
There are two photocopiable record sheets at the back of the Teacher's Resource Book and Pupils' Copymasters Book. We suggest you use these as follows.

Teacher's Resource Record Sheet 1: Photocopy one per child and record how many experiences relating to the skill sections each child has had. This is a matter for your own judgement. Some of the activities enable work to take place involving many aspects of Experimental and Investigative Science, others few. The kinds of enquiry that the children can undertake will depend also on how you set up the activity.

Sheet 2: Photocopy one per child, and record which parts of the Programme of Study the children have worked on.

Pupils' Copymaster Record Sheet 1: Photocopy one per child, and put a tick against those aspects of Experimental and Investigative Science which, in your judgement, the child has experienced in work they have recorded on the copymasters. There is a bar code containing the symbols we consider appropriate at the bottom of each copymaster to help you.

Sheet 2: Photocopy one per child and list the copymasters each child has worked on.

HOW TO USE THIS BOOK

If you have only the Teacher's Resource Book
You can use this book as a flexible resource which you can consult for ideas, activities and investigations to work on with children.

To use in class:
1 Consult the appropriate part of the Programme of Study reprinted at the start of each section.
2 Consider, in the light of the Programme of Study and your school records, the Areas of Study on which the children should be working.
3 Consult the appropriate parts of the section on Experimental and Investigative Science.
4 Within the chosen Areas of Study, select activities which best fit your management plans and resourcing.
5 Assemble the equipment which you and the children need to carry out the activities.
6 As each activity is completed, use Record Sheets 1 and 2 to record what the children have done.

If you also have the Pupils' Copymasters
7 Identify the appropriate copymasters and ensure that you have enough copies. There are notes on how to use the sheets in this book. You will find the appropriate sheets referred to in this book with this symbol:

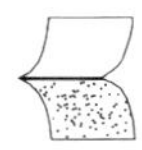

Give them to the children at the optimal time for them to do the necessary recording.
8 Use Record Sheets 1 and 2 to record what the children have done on the copymasters.

TOPIC PLANNER

If you wish to include science in your topic work, look down the following list of 20 common topic titles and identify any that are close to the topic that you are planning. Alongside the title we have indicated the location of Areas of Study in this book which support that topic. Depending on the emphasis of the work that you are planning, you may be able to incorporate Areas of Study other then those we have drawn attention to.

Topic title	Levels	Life processes and living things	Materials and their properties	Physical processes	Related topics
Families	2	1, 15			Animals Change Health
	3				
	4				
	5	27, 28			
Animals	2	2			Families Food Underground Seasons Health
	3	4, 5, 6			
	4	26, 34			
	5	29			
Food, nutrition and the environment	2	8			Animals Weather Water Seasons Health
	3	10			
	4	37			
	5				
Weather	2				Food Water Buildings Seasons Space
	3		4, 10		
	4		13		
	5				
Water	2	3		15	Food Weather
	3	18			
	4		13, 16		
	5		18	20	

Topic title	Levels	Life processes and living things	Materials and their properties	Physical processes	Related topics
Change	2	15, 21	8, 9		Families Buildings Time Seasons Space
	3	5, 6, 22	11, 12		
	4		14		
	5				
Our school	2	32			Buildings Seasons
	3	33			
	4				
	5				
Our village/ town	2	32			Buildings Seasons
	3				
	4				
	5				
The industrial revolution	2				Transport Buildings Time Communications
	3				
	4				
	5				
What is it made of?	2		1, 15		Underground Buildings Space
	3		2, 3		
	4		7		
	5		17		
Safety first	2				Health
	3				
	4				
	5				
Health/ feeling ill	2	7			Families Animals Food Safety
	3	9			
	4	11, 12, 14, 17			
	5	13			

Topic planner

Topic title	Levels	Life processes and living things	Materials and their properties	Physical processes	Related topics
Transport	2				Communications Industrial revolution
	3			6	
	4			11	
	5				
Underground	2	25	15		Animals What is it made of?
	3	38			
	4	20, 36	6		
	5	39			
Buildings	2				Weather Change Our school Our village/town Industrial revolution What is it made of?
	3				
	4			7	
	5				
Time	2				Buildings Seasons Communications Change Industrial revolution
	3				
	4	35		37	
	5			38, 39, 40, 41, 42	
Seasons	2				Animals Food Weather Time Change Our school Our village/town
	3	6	4		
	4				
	5				
Space	2			36	Weather Change What is it made of?
	3				
	4			37	
	5			38, 39, 40, 41, 42	
Communications	2				Transport Time Industrial revolution
	3				
	4			3	
	5				

Topic title	Levels	Life processes and living things	Materials and their properties	Physical processes	Related topics
The annual trip; castle, safari park, museum, etc.	2	Can cover all parts of the Programmes of Study and be related to most other topics, depending on where you go!			
	3				
	4				
	5				

BLUEPRINTS LINKS

You will find that the science work in this book can be supported by related cross-curricular activities and copymasters from other Junior and Key Stage 2 books. The index below gives references for related books which you may already have, or wish to acquire. Where a book contains a substantial bank of related material, the reference is given in italics.

The following books were revised in 1995 to match the revised National Curriculum, and all references for these books refer to the 1995 editions: *Blueprints: Maths, Science, English, History, Geography, Maths Investigations, Science Investigations.*

Section of National Curriculum Science Programme of Study

Life Processes and Living Things

1. Life processes
Easter: *complete topic on life cycles, topic on eggs;* **Junior Teacher's Resource Bank**: life cycles of a butterfly, frog and a human (copymasters 87–89).

2. Humans as organisms
Art Key Stage 1: topic on food and farming (pp. 39–47); **Easter**: human embryo (p. 55); **Environmental Education Key Stage 2**: how many breaths (p. 76), complete topic on food (pp. 93–110); **Health Education Key Stage 2**: *Teacher's Resource Book and Copymasters provide complete topics on growing up, medicines and drugs, exercising and healthy eating*; **Junior Geography Resource Bank**: food and crops (copymasters 62–67); **Junior Teacher's Resource Bank**: the human skeleton (copymaster 79), the digestive system (copymaster 80), life cycle of a human (copymaster 89); **Second Key Stage 2 Topics Book**: leisure (copymasters 1–3); **Science Investigations** (copymasters 4, 21, 26).

3. Green plants as organisms
Art Resource Bank: complete topic on flowers and plants; **Easter**: plant life cycles (p. 52); **Junior Geography Resource Bank**: growing rice (copymaster 65); **Junior Teacher's Resource Bank**: parts of a flower (copymaster 78), common trees and their leaves (copymaster 103); **Science Investigations** (copymasters 3, 25, 27, 31).

4. Variation and classification
Environmental Education Key Stage 2: a survey of a pond animal (p. 58), What is a tree? (p. 87), **Maths Key Stage 2**: Teacher's Resource Book, see Handling data section on sorting and classifying, carroll diagrams, tallying and frequency tables, tree diagrams, databases; **Maths Investigations**: whole school investigations (data day); **Science Investigations** (copymasters 2, 6, 71); **Topics Key Stage 2**: hot and cold (copymaster 1).

5. Living things in their environment
Environmental Education Key Stage 2: *food chains (p. 44), food web in a wood (p. 89), complete topic on waste (pp. 111–127), ocean food web (p. 158)*; **Junior Geography Resource Bank**: oak tree (copymaster 80); **Junior Teacher's Resource Bank**: animal homes 1 and 2 (copymasters 85–86), food chains (copymaster 96), habitats (copymaster 98); **Second Key Stage 2 Topics Book**: conservation (copymaster 7); **Science Investigations** (copymasters 1, 5, 20, 28).

Materials and Their Properties

1. Grouping and classifying materials
Junior Geography Resource Bank: rocks and soils (copymasters 33–39); **Maths Key Stage 2**: Teacher's Resource Book, see Handling data section on sorting and classifying, carroll diagrams, tallying and frequency tables, tree diagrams and databases; **Science Investigations** *(copymasters 8, 33, 37, 48, 50, 72, 75)*; **Technology Key Stage 2**: testing properties of materials (pp. 47–8), soil samples (p. 92), rocks (p. 93); **Topics Key Stage 2**: *complete topic on rocks and soil (pp. 19–37).*

2. Changing materials
Junior Geography Resource Bank: the water cycle (copymaster 15); **Junior Teacher's Resource Bank**: the water cycle (copymaster 102); **Science Investigations** (copymasters 7, 9, 13, 35, 88); **Technology Key Stage 2**: materials that change (pp. 22–24).

3. Separating mixtures of materials
Science Investigations (copymaster 36).

Physical Processes

1. Electricity
Junior Teacher's Resource Bank: generating electricity (copymaster 91); **Science Investigations** (copymasters 52, 64, 76, 82); **Technology Key Stage 2**: circuits 1 and 2 (pp. 10–11).

2. Forces and motion
Science Investigations *(copymasters 14, 16, 43, 45, 46, 47, 56, 57, 59, 60, 61, 65, 67, 74, 75, 78, 80, 84, 86)*; **Technology Key Stage 2**: systems 1 and 2 (pp. 5–6), controlling energy (pp. 7–9), levers (p. 14), pulleys 1 and 2 (pp. 15–16), water power (p. 17), wind energy (p. 18), flight (p. 19).

3. Light and sound
Art Key Stage 1: Teacher's Resource Book, complete topic on colour and light (copymasters 35–41, 97, 100); **Junior Teacher's Resource Bank**: inside the ear (copymaster 81), the eye (copymaster 82), the orchestra (copymaster 107); **Second Key Stage 2 Topics Book**: complete topic on sound (pp. 116–134); **Science Investigations** *(copymasters 10, 11, 15, 29, 30, 40, 41, 42, 44, 49, 53, 54, 55, 83, 91, 93, 94);* **Technology Key Stage 2**: light 1 and 2 (pp. 95–96), sound (pp. 99).

4. The Earth and beyond
Junior Teacher's Resource Bank: Earth in space (copymaster 90); **Second Key Stage 2 Topics Book**: *complete topic on space (pp. 135–154);* **Science Investigations** (copymaster 66); Topics Key Stage 2: hot and cold (copymasters 4–5).

COVERAGE OF THE CURRICULUM FOR SCOTLAND AND NORTHERN IRELAND

Blueprints: Science Key Stage 2 covers nearly all of the science requirements in place for 7–11-year-olds in Scotland and Northern Ireland. Most of those which are not covered – largely to do with personal health, weather and the environment – are present in other National Curriculum materials. You may find *Blueprints: Geography* Key Stage 2 and *Blueprints: Health Education* Key Stage 2 useful companion volumes.

In the chart below we have set out the key curriculum content of the relevant stages for Northern Ireland and Scotland. This has been cross-referenced to the Area of Study numbers in the three content areas of National Curriculum Science in this book, as follows:

- Life Processes and Living Things (**LP & LT**)
- Materials and Their Properties (**M & P**)
- Physical Processes (**PP**).

Links to Scottish National Science Guidelines (5–14)

Contexts and content for developing understanding (Stages P4–P6)

You will find the science contexts and content for P4–P6 science reproduced in shorthand form below.

Understanding living things	Areas of study in the book
Variety and characteristic features:	
• main distinguishing features of animal groups and plants;	**LP & LT**: partial coverage in 2, 3, 4, 23, 25, 26
• recognising members of these with keys;	**LP & LT**: 25, 26, 30, 31
• similarities and differences between plants and animals of the same species.	**LP & LT**: 29, 30, 31
The process of life:	
• Structure and functions of major body parts;	**LP & LT**: 7, 8, 9, 11, 12, 13, 14
• Structure and functions of parts of flowering plants;	**LP & LT**: 3, 5, 18, 19, 20, 21, 23, 24
• dispersal of fruits and seeds.	**LP & LT**: 22, 24
Interaction of living things with their environment:	
• interaction between humans and the environment;	
• simple food chains;	**LP & LT**: 37
• conservation and recycling;	**LP & LT**: 34, 36
• rare and extinct living things;	**LP & LT**: 34, 35
• environmental effects on plants and animals.	**LP & LT**: 32, 33, 34, 36

Understanding forces and energy	Areas of study in the book
Forms and sources of energy:	
• the Sun as a source of light and heat;	**PP**: 21, 28, 39
• sound from vibrating sources;	**PP**: 29–35
• electricity as a form of energy;	**PP**: 1–7
• sources of electricity.	
Properties and uses of energy:	
• use of thermometers to measure 'hotness';	**M & P**: 10
• sunlight and shadows;	**PP**: 23, 27, 37, 40
• mirrors and reflections;	**PP**: 25, 26
• lenses;	
• colours in sunlight;	
• applications of mirrors and lenses;	**PP**: 26
• pitch and volume;	**PP**: 29–35
• electrical conductors and insulators;	**M & P**: 5
• construction of battery-operated circuits;	**PP**: 1–7
• electrical safety.	
Conversion and transfer of energy:	
• forms of energy can be converted.	
Forces and their effects:	
• friction forces;	**PP**: 11
• air resistance;	**PP**: 11
• forces of gravity;	**PP**:10
• magnetic materials.	**M & P**: 1; **PP**: 8, 9

Understanding Earth and Space	Areas of study in the book
Earth in space:	
• planets and the solar system;	**PP**: 36
• measuring passage of time.	**PP**: 37, 39, 40, 42
On planet Earth:	
• the Earth's atmosphere;	
• the water cycle;	**M & P**: 11, 13
• patterns of weather.	
Materials from Earth:	
• uses of water – water conservation;	
• properties of common materials;	**M & P**: 1, 2, 4, 5, 7, 16, 17, 18
• natural and manufactured materials;	**PP**: 1, 3
• how materials can be changed.	**PP**: 8, 9, 11, 12, 13, 14

Links to the Northern Ireland Science Curriculum for Key Stage 2
(You will find the key Programme of Study points for AT2–4 from the 1992 document produced below in short-hand form.)

Links with AT2: Living things	Areas of study in the book
• investigate two localities	**LP & LT**: 36
• environmental effects on plants and animals	**LP & LT**: 32–36
• decay	**LP & LT**: 38, 39
• life-forms as fossils	**LP & LT**: 34, 35
• identify plants and animals with keys	**LP & LT**: 25–31
• function of the major organ systems	**LP & LT**: 7–9, 11–14
• promotion of good health	**LP & LT**: 7–10, 13, 17
• physical factors and rate of plant growth	**LP & LT**: 18–21

Links with AT3: Materials	Areas of study in the book
• characteristics of everyday materials	**M & P**: 1, 2, 4, 5, 7, 16–18
• uses of materials	**M & P**: 2–4
• liquids and gases	**M & P**: 7
• the water cycle	**M & P**: 11, 13
• acidic, alkaline and neutral solutions	
• changes in materials and new materials produced	**M & P**: 11–12, 14
• warming, cooling, evaporating and condensing	**M & P**: 9, 11

Links with AT4: Forces and energy	Areas of study in the book
• food is essential for life	
• hot and cold in relation to body temperature	**M & P**: 10
• heating and cooling substances	**M & P**: 11–12
• investigating a range of fuels	
• energy storage and self-propelled devices	**PP**: 12
• energy transfer	
• friction and gravity	**PP**: 10–11
• forces and presence of forces in road safety	**PP**: 13–20
• floating and sinking	**PP**: 20
• constructing circuits	**PP**: 1–7
• dangers of electricity	
• measuring electrical consumption	
• magnetic and non-magnetic properties	**PP**: 8–9
• how sounds are produced and heard	**PP**: 29–30, 34

Links with AT4: Forces and energy	Areas of study in the book
• how sound travels through different materials	**PP**: 31–33
• pitch and volume	**PP**: 35
• light passing through transparent things	**PP**: 23
• shadows	**PP**: 23, 27, 37, 40
• mirrors	**PP**: 22, 26
• how light behaves	**PP**: 21–27

Links with AT5: Environment	Areas of study in the book
• study the effects of human activity on the environment	
• raw materials, waste disposal and decay	**LP & LT**: 38–39
• waste materials and recycling	
• changes in the night sky	**PP**: 38, 41
• day and night, year length, aspects of the Moon	**PP**: 37–40, 42
• relative position of the Sun, Moon and Earth	**PP**: 36, 41, 42

COMMON REQUIREMENTS OF THE PROGRAMME OF STUDY

The requirements in this section of the Programme of Study apply across Experimental and investigative science, Life processes and living things, Materials and their properties and Physical processes.

In order to make this section of the Programme of Study more accessible, we have given examples of activities which relate to each of the points stated. The activities are drawn from other sections of this book. They provide opportunities to develop the necessary areas of knowledge. Also, where appropriate, additional activities have been included here to help the children to master a range of scientific skills.

1. Systematic enquiry

Pupils should be given opportunities to:

a ask questions related to their work in science;

> *Life processes and living things:* Area of study 6, Activity 1
> *Physical processes:* Area of study 20, Activity 1

b use focused exploration and investigation to acquire scientific knowledge, understanding and skills;

> *Life processes and living things:* Area of study 33, Activity 1
> *Materials and their properties:* Area of study 4, Activity 2
> *Physical processes:* Area of study 4, Activity 1

c use both first-hand experience and secondary sources to obtain information;

> *Life processes and living things:* Area of study 26, Activity 2
> *Physical processes:* Area of study 11, Activity 5

d use IT to collect, store, retrieve and present scientific information.

> *Life processes and living things:* Area of study 26, Activity 3

IT in schools

A wide range of computing and sensing equipment is now available in schools, ranging from calculators to computers, and tape recorders to electronic sensors. Because experience in handling information using technology can be episodic in school, we feel it is a skill area in which teachers may want to place extra activities, giving skill practice. We have set out some suggested activities in the following pages.

P of S 1d

SENDING MESSAGES

C1

Purpose
To demonstrate that messages can be transmitted in a number of ways.

Materials needed
Second timers, information about heraldry, badges and flags.

Activity 1: Messages using human body and voice
Take the children into the playground. Let each of them find a partner. Then tell the whole group that they are going to try a number of ways of getting a message to their friend. Let each pair label themselves A and B. Get the Bs to stand in a line on the far side of the playground. Brief the As' that they are to stay in a line opposite their partner and give them a message by running to whisper it in their ear. Then get them to shout it, and finally let them signal it across the playground. Reverse the As and Bs so that everyone has a turn at message-taking. Discuss which method seemed the most efficient and why.

Divide the children into an even number of small groups with about four children in each group. Give each group a 'name', e.g. a colour or a letter. Pair off the groups so that each is working with another group. Let one group of each pair stand at one side of the playground with their partner group on the opposite side. Let one group of each pair confer to decide how they will deliver a message to their partner group. As you give them a message, get them to start the timer. See how long it takes and whether this method allows accurate delivery.

Activity 2: Codes
Discuss simple codes for messages. The children will have some ideas from their attempts at signalling in Activity 1. Let the children invent codes based on colours, shapes and movement, e.g. arm or leg positions. Look at and discuss the codes behind, for example, traffic-lights, heraldry, the school badge and flags flown by ships. The children can have fun encoding and decoding messages. Their codes can be written up in book form and displayed.

Activity 3: Sending long-distance messages
Look at the everyday ways of sending messages over a long distance, including letters, telephone calls and television. Arrange to exchange letters with a similar class in another school. Discuss the way we set up the message, how we pay for delivery and the route the message takes. Work out the time between posting and delivery.

Discuss the advantages and disadvantages of making a telephone call, compared with sending a letter.

Talk about the two-way possibilities in letters and telephone calls and compare these with television messages which are one-way.

Use copymaster 1 for the children to record the routes taken by a letter and a telephone message.

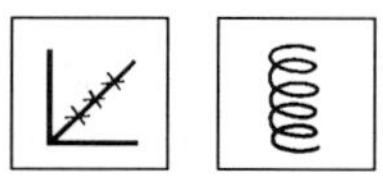

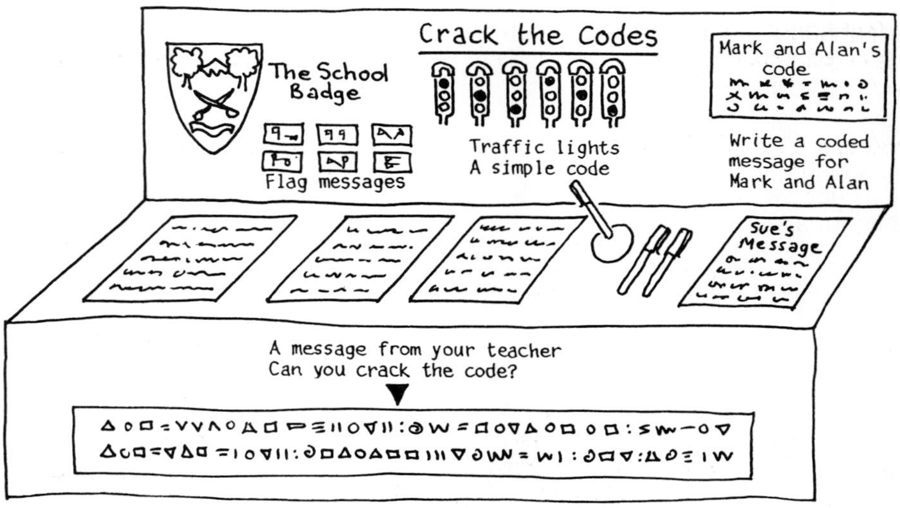

P of S 1d

INFORMATION STORAGE

Purpose
To show that information can be stored in a variety of ways.

Materials needed
Access to school library; telephone directories, used envelopes addressed to the children's families; maps.

Activity 1: School library
Look round the school library with the children. Ask them to try to find out how it is arranged. Are the books arranged alphabetically, by author, by topic, subject or size? Then discuss how you find the information you are looking for. Give the children some puzzle questions to see if they can 'access the information store' (i.e. look up the answers).

Activity 2: Telephone directories
Show the children what is contained in a directory. Let them look up their own telephone number, that of a friend, the police station, library and others. Show the children what local codes are, and what national and international codes look like.

Activity 3: Postcodes
Get the children to bring in a used envelope addressed to their family, with the postcode on it. Using a map of the locality, and postcode information found in some telephone directories, plot the location of postcodes, and discuss what information is therefore 'stored' in a postcode.

Activity 4: Maps
Let the children study a map key, identify some of the symbols and seek them out on the map. The map is an information 'store'.

P of S 1d

ELECTRONIC STORAGE OF INFORMATION

C2

Purpose
To show that electronic devices can be used to store information, and to access some information.

Materials needed
Tape recorders with cassettes, photo albums or folders, digital watches, calculators, video cameras with film and playback machine, computer and software, packages with bar codes on them, access to a telephone.

Activity 1: Using tape recorders
Show the children how to load a cassette, make a recording and replay it. Let the children work in pairs, making tape recordings of each other, sound effects and interviews. When they are skilled at producing a good recording, let them decide on a topic of current interest, or where a tape recording is an asset. They can then create a written/audio record of their topic, and they can present it in a photo album or folder.

Activity 2: Tape recorders: sound effects
Let the children record sound effects around the school, e.g. footsteps, creaking doors, rain on the roof, a running tap, and then use these sounds as a resource for drama lessons.

Activity 3: Digital watches
Let the children use a digital watch and set a time-limit to an activity marked by an alarm.

Activity 4: Bar codes
Discuss what these mean and how they are used in supermarkets.

Activity 5: Speaking clock
Let the children ring the speaking clock, and then discuss how it operates. Explain to them that it works on a radio signal from an atomic clock.

Activity 6: Children's use of information stores
Let the children list their own uses of electronic information stores, including the phone with a number memory, pelican crossings, computer games, video-recorders.

Activity 7: Calculators
Use electronic calculators to play a variety of number games. Give the children the chance to use memory, memory recall and iteration. (Choose calculators that do not round up automatically and will iterate, i.e. when you key **x+y=** and continue pressing **+**, **y** is repeatedly added on.)

Activity 8: School video
A real store of information that the children will understand can be made by arranging with other staff and your headteacher and class that you film a day in the life of a group of children. The video is part of school archives, as the children will realise when you show it to them after a couple of years.

Activity 9: Videos
Help the children to write scripts and storyboards for a short video about some aspect of their work. Film it and play back. Add to school resources.

Copymaster 2 can be used for a storyboard layout.

Activity 10: Computers
Show the children how to load software and access it themselves.

Let the children play computer games and store their entries or scores.

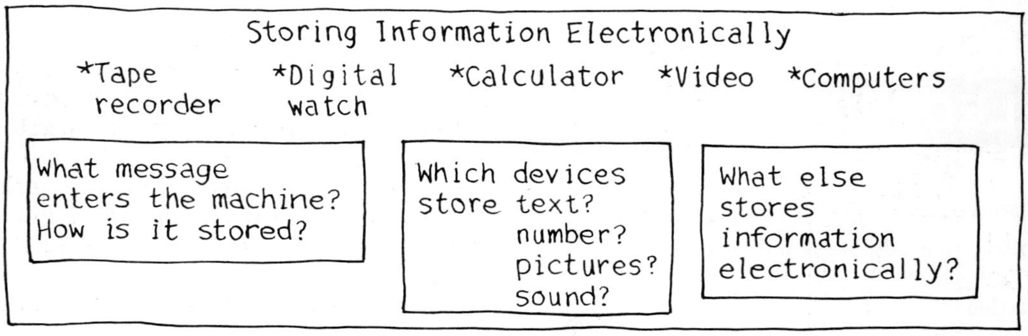

P of S 1d RETRIEVAL OF INFORMATION

Purpose
To be able to retrieve information stored on a computer.

Materials needed
Computer and database, graphics and sounds software.

Activity 1: Retrieval of text and numbers
Use a commercially-produced package, bought with the advice of county advisers, with which children can access information. Give them puzzle questions which they can only answer by accessing the appropriate information. Databases made by children in the school can also be used.

Activity 2: Creation of and retrieval from database
Show the children how to create and use a database to organise information. Either create a database about the children themselves, or about something that interests them, such as cars, TV personalities, storybook heroes and heroines or space facts. The children should learn how to put the information in and know how to access it in a variety of ways.

Activity 3: Computer graphics
Use a graphics package to show children what can be done on screen. Let them use the package and print out their efforts. Some exciting and comparatively inexpensive art packages are now available.

Activity 4: Computer sound
Use a software package with sound effects, so that children can get computer sound feedback. There are music packages available with which children can play and be creative.

P of S 1d ENVIRONMENTAL CHANGE

Purpose
To show how to measure changes in the environment using a variety of instruments.

Materials needed
Tape recorders and cassettes, light meter, camera with built in light meter and film, access to school boiler room or central heating control room; advertising material about electronic heating control, Celsius thermometers, electronic sensor which measures temperature.

Activity 1: Sound levels
Together with the children, plan and record the sounds of a school day. The children may wish to try controlling a selection of variables, and they could work in groups

to devise a recording sequence where, for example, the location is fixed, they record only voices, or they record only noises outside school which may impinge, such as those made by aircraft, traffic or roadworks. They may choose to be selective, to match their sound track to a journalistic account of the school day, or they may fix a time interval between recordings and look at changes in noise levels. In groups they should be able to plan and execute an experiment and then give a presentation of results.

Activity 2: Light levels
Let the children use a light meter at a fixed location in the classroom to detect changes in light levels during a school day. If the children use a light meter that is built into a camera, and take a photo at each light check, you will need to discuss with them the connection between the size of aperture and available light.

Activity 3: Temperature control
Find out how the school heating system works. Ask the caretaker to show the children the boilers and the controls, including thermostats. Look through advertising material about electronic heating system thermostats, available from electricity and gas showrooms and appliance shops.

Activity 4: Temperature change
Let the children use an electronic sensor in a fixed location, to check the classroom temperature throughout a school day. They can record temperature changes and comment in writing on how they can account for the changes over the day, which may include things such as school heating, position of the Sun, open windows and doors, presence or absence of people and so on.

Copymaster 3 can be used to record these observations.

2. Science in everyday life

Pupils should be given opportunities to:

a use their knowledge and understanding of science to explain and interpret a range of familiar phenomena;

Life processes and living things: Area of study 38, Activity 3
Physical processes: Area of study 37, Activity 1

b consider the part science has played in the development of many of the things that they use;

Materials and their properties: Area of study 12, Activity 3
Physical processes: Area of study 29, Activity 1

c relate their understanding of science to their personal health;

Life processes and living things: Area of study 9, Activity 1

d consider ways in which living things and the environment need protection.

Life processes and living things: Area of study 34, Activity 4

The following activities could be used as a means of introducing **2c**.

P of S 2c LOOKING AFTER YOURSELF

Purpose
To persuade children to do certain important things for their health.

Materials needed
A wash bag and contents; empty food packages from all the main food groups; trainers and PE kit along with, for example, a skipping-rope and ball; a pillow and bedding or a made up doll's bed.

Activity 1: Personal hygiene
Discuss cleanliness and examine the contents of the wash bag, which may include soap, flannel, toothbrush and paste. Start a display with these items.

Activity 2: Healthy eating
Talk about the four main food groups: proteins, carbohydrates, fats and vitamins and minerals. Discuss what we should eat every day for health. Mention some of the foods which we should avoid or have only occasionally. Ask the children to bring in the packaging for healthy foods belonging to the four groups and add these to the display started in Activity 1.

Activity 3: Keeping fit
Discuss the importance of exercise to keep healthy and examine the trainers, PE kit and exercise aids (rope, ball) to fuel the discussion, and to get the children talking about appropriate kit for exercise and equipment which helps us to exercise. Add these to the display.

Activity 4: Sleep and rest
Display the bedding or doll's bed, having discussed the importance of rest and sleep.

These activities aim to develop the children's knowledge relating to **2d**.

P of S 2d CLASSIFICATION OF WASTE

C4

Purpose
To identify which kinds of waste can be safely put back into the land and which cannot be disposed of in this way.

Materials needed
Plastic, paper and metal waste samples; a spade, an earthernware flowerpot; cartons and bottles with a 'green' label, to compare with similar products which lack this label.

Activity 1: Testing what is biodegradable
Bury a piece of plastic bag, a can and a piece of paper in a carefully marked spot in the school garden or in an earthenware flowerpot which is then put outside. Leave it for as long as possible – at least half a term. Unearth what you have buried and observe and record what has happened.

The experimental results can be recorded pictorially and in writing on copymaster 4.

Activity 2: Packaging: what is biodegradable?
Compare washing-up liquid bottles, washing powder packets and other packaging carrying a biodegradable label with similar packaging which does not. Discuss with the children the responsibility of the manufacturer and consumer in 'choosing green'.

P of S 2d HUMANS AND THE EARTH'S SURFACE C5

Purpose
To demonstrate that humans change the local landscape.

Materials needed
Information related to local development projects or building projects, drawing paper and pencils, camera and film; books on arable farming.

Activity 1: Observing the changes humans make
This activity will depend on the location of your school and plans in the area. The reclamation of coastline, the building of a section of motorway or a housing estate might be taking place near to you. Any of these projects can be watched over time. If there are no such projects nearby or if trips out are not possible, then you will have to collect (in advance) a dossier of pictures about a project, and 'before' and 'after' pictures of the landscape. It is possible that maps and street plans may show these changes. The children can construct 'before' and 'after' models of that piece of landscape.

If you wish, the children can draw a view of the landscape before and after the changes on copymaster 5.

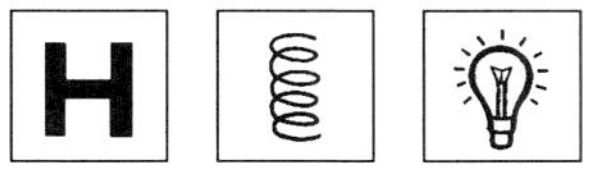

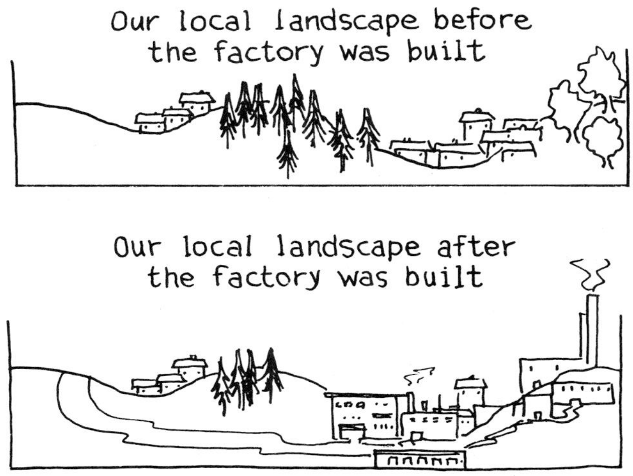

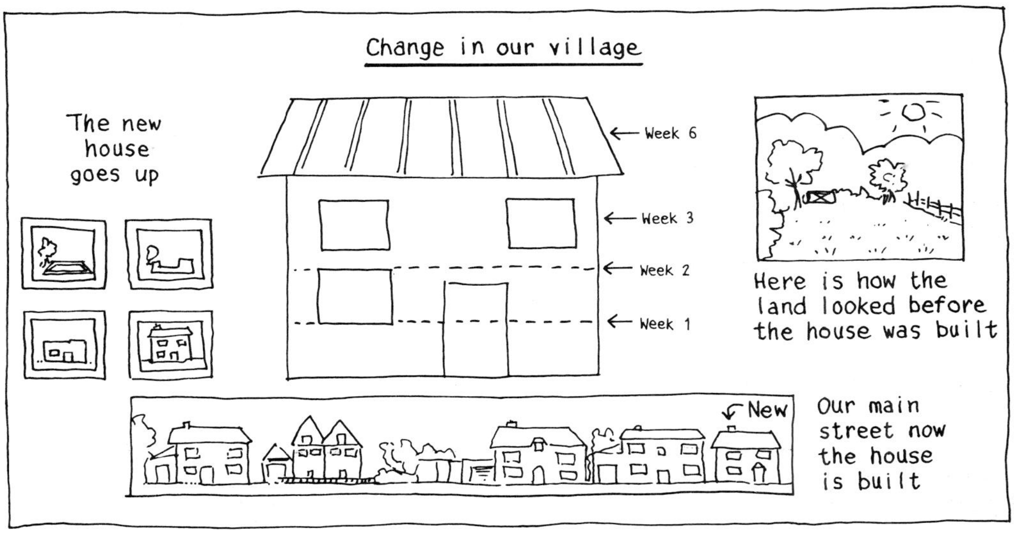

Activity 2: A new building seen as environmental change
If possible let the children observe the erection of a new building, by taking them along to look and draw the changes every few days. You will need to arrange this with the owner of the property, and the senior person on site. Also, do make sure that the children stand at a safe distance to watch. Their drawings can be displayed, and you can trace over one set and superimpose each stage on top of the other to show the 'growth' of the building over time. If you take some photographs too, the children can see the effects of the alterations on the whole street.

Activity 3: Local use of land
Look with the children at the use made of the land locally. If you work in an inner-city school take the children to the nearest open country, or if this is not possible go and take photographs of the local landscape. Let the children look at maps of the area, and list and talk about what human beings are doing to the land. There may be positive effects of the work of humans, including some of the following examples:

- Organic farming
- Preservation schemes, tree renewal and hedge maintenance
- Landscaping of tips and slag heaps

- Creation of new features like reservoirs (some people may see this as a negative effect, particularly as natural habitats and features are destroyed).

There may also be negative effects of the work of humans, including some of the following:

- Deforestation
- Unsightly quarries, industrial sites and rubbish tips
- Chemical intervention in attempts to improve crop yields
- Destruction of 'natural countryside' in the construction of golf courses and other leisure activity sites
- Motorway construction.

Activity 4: The farmer's year
Visit a local farm with the children during each of the four seasons of the year. The children can create a 'farmer's diary' for a typical year, listing changes in what a farmer does as the year passes. If the children cannot see a farmer at work, consult books about farming and let them draw what they think an arable farmer does to the land over the passage of a year.

P of S 2d FERTILISERS AND THE ENVIRONMENT C6

Purpose
To formulate opinions about fertilisers and the environment, and to get the children to back up their arguments with information based on their own experience.

Materials needed
A list of the constituents of some fertilisers, letter-writing materials.

Activity 1: Fertilisers and agriculture
Either visit a farm where chemical fertilisers are used, or invite a farmer to visit you. Observe and discuss the changes made by chemical fertilisers.

Activity 2: Production of fertilisers
Write to a major producer of fertilisers and ask them for publicity material about their range of natural and manufactured products. Examine and discuss the implications of the advertising material.

Activity 3: Organic farming and gardening
Visit an organic garden. Find out what is done to get a good yield and what problems there are.

Copymaster 6 can be used for consolidation.

DE

P of S 2d HUMANS AND THE AIR

Purpose
To show that humans pollute the Earth's atmosphere.

Materials needed
Pictures of factory chimneys emitting smoke and fumes; publicity material about petrol fumes and unleaded petrol; anti-smoking leaflets.

Activity: Clean air
Look at the available information with the children and discuss its implications. The children can devise their own 'clean air' posters for display.

Pollution changes our world and us

P of S 2d HUMANS, RIVERS AND COASTAL WATERS

Purpose
To show that waste humans create is being discharged into rivers and seas, causing pollution.

Materials needed
A nearby river or stream, river monitoring station, or a strip of coastline with an accessible high-tide mark;

rubbish bags and a large jar for a water sample, rubber gloves; a visitor from a 'clean up rivers' organisation; books about the state of our rivers.

Activity 1: River or sea inspection
If you are lucky enough to live near a suitable river or on the coast, the children can take a stretch of river or shoreline, perhaps about 10m long, and firstly look at its general features, then at what lives and grows there. Then they can collect any rubbish there is and a sample of water. Back in the classroom they can collate their findings, examine, draw and weigh the rubbish and inspect the water. Remember there may be health risks here, so supply rubber gloves if necessary. Their resulting work can be displayed, and if their results are alarming, they could be sent to the owners of the water or land for their attention.

Activity 2: River monitoring
Invite someone from the river's authority to come and talk to the children about measures which are being taken to clean up the rivers.

P of S 2d

IMPROVING THE ENVIRONMENT

C7

Purpose
To devise and adopt a scheme for improving the environment.

Materials needed
Garden tools, seeds and plants, rubbish bags; a range of waste packaging, including cardboard, plastic, cans, newspapers and bottles.

Activity 1: The school garden
With the head and governors' permission, take over a plot in the school garden and transform it into, for example, a scented garden, a garden attracting butterflies or a wild flower garden. There may be capitation money or PTA money to finance this, or a local garden centre may sponsor you. If there is no land available belonging to the school, you can use plant troughs and large pots to produce miniature gardens. If you start a project like this, be prepared to put in much extra time yourself. The children will be keen and willing, but will find it difficult to be enthusiastic about routine weeding. The progress of the project can be monitored by the children themselves, and their resulting work can be displayed to advantage. It can also become a continuing school resource and a school garden log-book can be started, which will be added to by succeeding generations of children.

Activity 2: Litter campaign
With your help the children can mark out a cluster of roads near the school. With adult help, they can scour the pavements, kerbs and hedges for litter. The resulting haul (collected in black rubbish bags) can be placed where all can see. The children can combine this result with a request to local householders about litter. With adult help leaflets can be distributed. Every child in the school can be given one to take home. This would be a suitable 'project' for a school video.

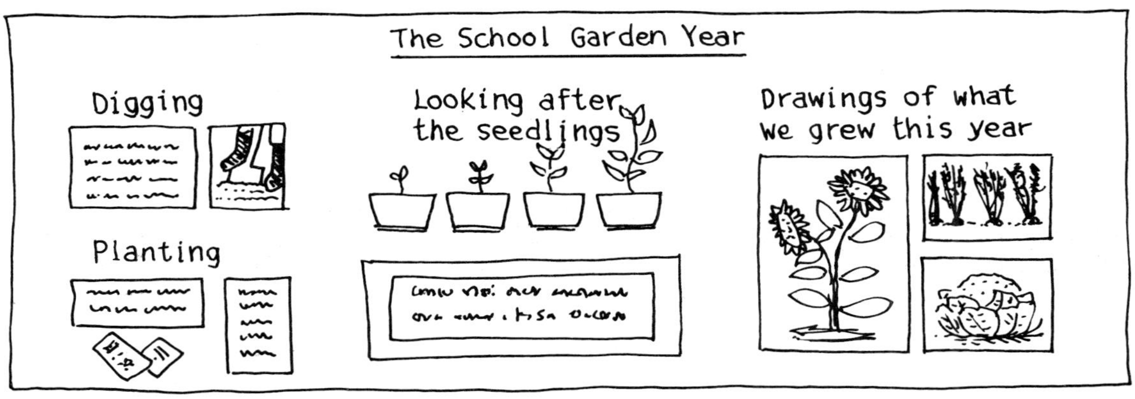

Activity 3: Discussion and sorting of waste
Remind the children that some packaging can be re-cycled. Talk about bottle banks and newspaper collection points. Ask them if they can offer to assemble these things regularly in their own home, ready for a trip to local collection points.

The children can make a collection of re-usable waste for a specified fortnight at home, and when they have collected it all, record how much of each kind of waste is produced.

The recording can be done on copymaster 7.

Activity 4: Official recycling
Ask the local department of environmental health if it is possible for someone to come and speak to the children about what happens to household waste – what can be recycled and how.

Activity 5: Supermarket packaging
With the co-operation of a local supermarket, ask if you and the children may look at and list the packaging materials found in a typical supermarket trolley of shopping. The supermarket manager may be helpful if your visit can receive publicity in the local paper. The children can work out how much packaging is recyclable.

P of S 2d

ALL ISSUES IN POLLUTION

Purpose
To explain humans' responsibility for pollution, its causes and outcomes.

Materials needed
Information about pollution from a wide range of sources including the Green party and protest groups; books and posters, tape recorders.

Activity 1: In-depth study of a kind of pollution
Ask the children to choose to study either the pollution of the air, the water or the land. They can then research this topic and produce a description of pollutants, their effects and an action list on preventing pollution. This work can be put into a folder for display. They can also write a personal statement about preventing this pollution and read this speech to the class, or record it on tape for their classmates to go and listen to.

Activity 2: The pollution debate
Ask the children to assemble information on one side or the other of a pollution issue, e.g. *against* smoking/ *for* individual choice; *against* discharge of industrial effluent into rivers/ *for* controlled discharge. Convene a formal debate to air both sides of the issue. The main arguments for and against each issue can be recorded on the two sides of a stand-up display which can be read from either side. Place it in the centre of the room so that the children can walk around it.

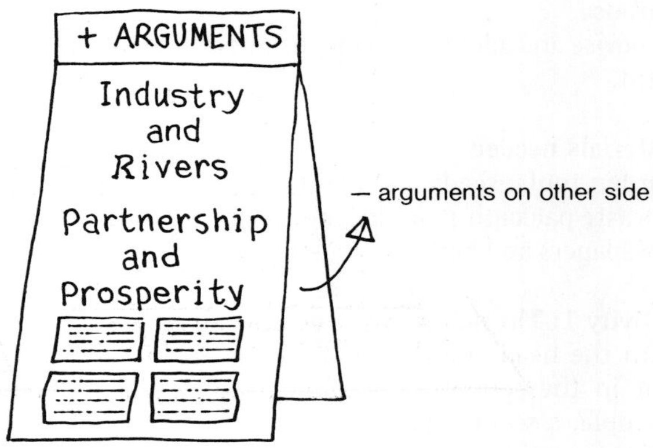

P of S 2d

PLANNING AND POLLUTION

C8

Purpose
To identify and explain the issues both for and against a planning proposal.

Materials needed
Information about real planning proposals (local if possible). News about the outcomes of the submission of such proposals. Newspaper reports of projects having environmental impact, from initial plan to final implementation, tape recorders and a video camera, if available and appropriate.

Activity 1: Role-play: enquiry into an imaginary plan
Tell the children that they are to pretend a plan has been put before the local council to build, for example, a toy factory on the school playing field, or to take out the hedges round the school and replace them with 10m high metal fencing. The kind of plan you choose will depend on the location and appearance of your school. Some of the children can be local councillors, others residents, including children. Let the children assemble as many arguments as they can about their point of view and then role-play the enquiry. If appropriate, the proceedings can be recorded or put on video. Several children can also take minutes and write up a report on the enquiry.

If you wish, the people to be called to the enquiry can use copymaster 8 to record a character description, their vested interests, and arguments they are going to make.

DE

Activity 2: The course of a genuine planning enquiry
This activity involves research and detective work, both on your part and the children's. Collection of information will take place over a long period of time. The children can then assemble a summary of the plan, a list of all the arguments put forward on either side and a summary of the outcomes. If the plan is current and affects the immediate environment of the school, you may like to approach some local residents to see if they would be willing to come into school and be interviewed about their views on the plans. The interviews can be recorded and added to the school's resources.

P of S 2d

NOISE CONTROL

C9, 10

Purpose
To understand that we can and should sometimes reduce noise or minimise its effects.

Materials needed
A Walkman®, industrial earmuffs, tape recorders.

Activity 1: Noise we make
Explain the dangers of having the volume control on a Walkman® turned up, and the nuisance it causes to other people (e.g. when on a bus or train). Discuss also the noise pollution that aircraft, cars and motor bikes can cause, and what we can do to effect change.

Copymaster 9 gives children the opportunity to write about noise that annoys. They can choose a local noise problem such as aircraft noise or write about noises they themselves hate.

Activity 2: Industrial noise
Discuss the necessity for some workers to take precautions against noise by wearing earmuffs, e.g. those on tractors or using road drills and in some factories.

Activity 3: Measuring noise levels
Using the experience the children may have had in *Environmental change,* Activity 1, pages 4–5, get them to design a noise investigation experiment and carry it out, using tape recorders. They may, for example, decide to record the noise at various events at school, e.g. in the playground, in the dining hall, in assembly. Alternatively they may wish to look at extraneous noise affecting them in school, e.g. roadworks, or heavy traffic.

Copymaster 10 presents a suggested framework for a noise investigation.

3. The nature of scientific ideas

Pupils should be given opportunities to:

a obtain evidence to test scientific ideas in a variety of ways;

Life processes and living things: Area of study 25, Activity 1

b recognise that science provides explanations for many phenomena.

Materials and their properties: Area of study 9, Activity 5
Physical processes: Area of study 8, Activity 1

4. Communication

Pupils should be taught to:

a use appropriate scientific vocabulary to describe and explain the behaviour of living things, materials and processes;

Materials and their properties: Area of study 11, Activity 2

b use standard measures and SI units, *e.g. metre, newton,* appropriate to their work;

Physical processes: Area of study 19, Activity 4

c use a wide range of methods, including diagrams, drawings, graphs, tables and charts, to record and present information in an appropriate and systematic manner.

5. Health and safety

Pupils should be given opportunities to:

a recognise and assess the hazards and risks to themselves and to others when working with living things and materials.

b take action to control these risks.

Materials and their properties: Area of study 11, Activity 4

These activities apply directly to **5a** and **5b**, and it is important for all the children to complete them.

P of S
5a, b

HOME AND ROAD SAFETY

C11

Purpose
To inform children of dangers in the home and near roads.

Materials needed
Booklets about road safety (including a road floor mat and toys or a local road map). Information about 'stranger danger'. Books about safety in the home, the danger of empty medicine bottles, etc.

Activity: Staying safe
A project on safety on the roads, 'stranger danger' and staying safe in the home can take weeks to study. If you wish to study it in depth (e.g. because the children seem unaware of the important issues) then try a cross-curricular topic which will meet some of the requirements of other subjects. A road safety project can involve the construction of a road scene on the playmat, or older children could mark the road hazards on a local road map. 'Stranger danger' can be covered with the help of a visit from a police officer.

Safety in the home raises many important points about which children should be informed, including toys left on the floor, electricity, naked flames, hot pans and kettles and medicines. Create a 'safety at home' display.

Use copymaster 11 for children to picture record.

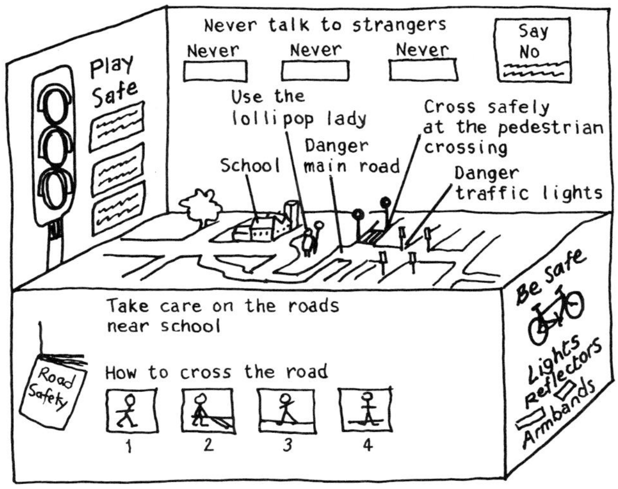

P of S 5a, b

SAFETY AND MATERIALS

Purpose
To discuss the fact that certain materials should be handled with care.

Materials needed
Examples of cleaning materials.

Activity: Safety and everyday materials
This discussion needs to be handled so that the children are not made over-anxious. Talk about taking care with everyday materials. Explain, for example, the dangers of boiling water and hot oil (which is very hot indeed – much hotter than boiling water). Point out that many items in the cleaning cupboard at home may be harmful to the skin, let alone our insides and should NEVER be smelled or tasted. Most cleaning powders and creams affect sensitive skin. Children should be encouraged to avoid them unless they have a grown up helping or watching.

P of S 5a, b

ELECTRICITY: DANGERS AND SAFETY

C12

Purpose
To show that electricity can be dangerous, and to provide advice on how to avoid hazards.

Materials needed
Books and publicity material related to the dangers of electricity and the correct use of home appliances; photographs of lightning.

Activity 1: Hazards at home
Look at the books and leaflets with the children and discuss the hazards of electricity at home, including trailing flex, electricity points accessible to small children, water near appliances. Let the children check their homes JUST BY LOOKING, and report back to their parents and teachers on the possible sources of hazard.

The children can complete copymaster 12 to record some of these hazards.

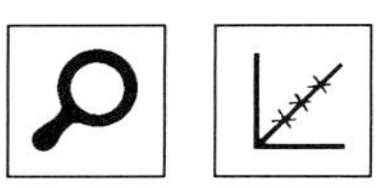

Activity 2: Hazards at school
Groups of children, accompanied by an adult, can tour the school looking for sources of electrical hazard; e.g. are sockets loose, plugs ill-fitting, flexes on appliances worn? Are there appliances near water (e.g. the kettle on the staffroom draining board)? They should draw or write where there are hazards, and report orally to the headteacher.

Activity 3: Hazards in the kitchen
The school cook may be able to talk to the children about all the care he/she has to take with electricity. He/she may be able to point out the sources of danger in the school kitchen while showing the children round.

Activity 4: Static electricity
Discuss with the children the sensation of a shock from the static in vigorously brushed hair, nylon petticoats and some jumpers. Explain that lightning is electricity which sometimes creates sparks and can set fire to trees.

Activity 5: Danger logos
Let the children design danger logos and create posters and charts about electricity. A safety display can be created.

Experimental and investigative science

Programme of study

Contexts derived from Life processes and living things, Materials and their properties and Physical processes should be used to teach pupils about experimental and investigative methods. On some occasions, the whole process of investigating an idea should be carried out by pupils themselves.

Pupils should be taught:

1. Planning experimental work

a to turn ideas suggested to them and their own ideas, into a form that can be investigated;

b that making predictions can be useful when planning what to do;

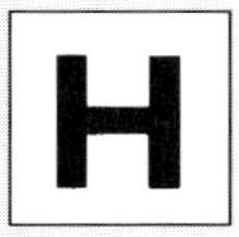

c to decide what evidence should be collected;

d that changing one factor and observing or measuring the effect, whilst keeping other factors the same, allows a fair test or comparison to be made;

e to consider what apparatus and equipment to use.

2. Obtaining evidence

a to use simple apparatus and equipment correctly;

b to make careful observations and measurements;

c to check observations and measurements by repeating them.

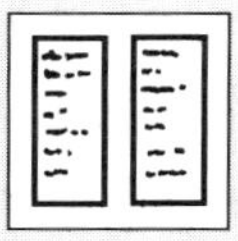

3. Considering evidence

a to use tables, bar charts and line graphs to present results;

b to make comparisons and to identify trends or patterns in results;

c to use results to draw conclusions;

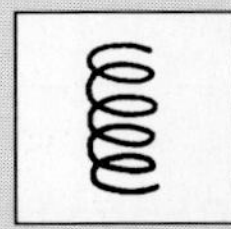

d to indicate whether the evidence collected supports any prediction made;

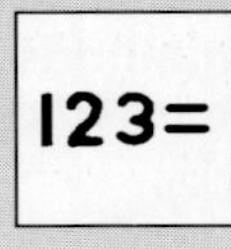

e to try to explain conclusions in terms of scientific knowledge and understanding.

Notes on this section of the Programme of Study

This section is all about scientific method: those investigative skills that all scientists use. In summary form they include the following:

- formulating hypotheses and making predictions
- 'fair tests'
- using measuring equipment
- systematic result checking and recording
- searching for patterns
- data interpretation, evaluation and explanation.

Below is a commentary on each of the skills in turn. You may choose to meet these skill requirements by either:

- doing activities planned with skill acquisition as the objective, or
- doing substantive activities where, aside from the knowledge they gain, children can be introduced to or practise skills. (To help with this we have already identified experimental and investigative science skills using symbols.)

Formulating testable hypotheses

Unlike our day-to-day problem-solving, which does not have to be systematic, scientific method requires that we continually attempt to confirm or discredit our theories by putting forward new ideas that can be tested out both by us and other people. Children can be helped to think of ideas that conform to these rules.

'Fair tests'

The concept of a 'fair test' is central to scientific method. Controlling variables and making objective comparisons is the way in which scientists work. Children need to understand that science relies on measurable comparisons which are not altered by prejudice, luck or inaccurate work. A 'fair test' has these characteristics:

- Control of variables
- A series of observations
- Stated accuracy of observation/measurement.

We carry out experiments to see what happens when things in our world change. Factors that have to do with the changes are called variables. Children need to begin their learning by identifying salient variables. They should, with experience, become skilled at suggesting ways these might be controlled and measured.

Using measuring equipment

Scientific method has rigorous rules about how ideas should be set out and tested. There are also rules about the appropriate use of equipment. Children need to know about working safely, taking care of equipment, choosing equipment which is appropriate for the kind of task in hand and taking measurements carefully. The range is from measuring jugs, rulers and spring balances to electronic sensors and microscopes. The kinds of decisions appropriate for the children are these:

- What can we measure?
- How best can it be measured?
- How many measurements do we need?
- How accurate are my measurements?

Checking and recording data

It is part of scientific method to be patient and painstaking in collecting data and thorough, scrupulous and systematic in recording, organising and presenting it. Through guided practice from simple lists through to charts and tables children should be helped to make decisions about how they set about putting data on paper or the computer. The National Curriculum Statutory Orders for Using and Applying Mathematics are also helpful in establishing data organising skills in children. Consult them to find ways of linking skills in maths and science.

Data patterns

Successful and systematic collection and recording of data make it possible to look for pattern. A pattern of data is essential for us to pose an explanation for what happens in an experiment. Even chance discovery in the history of science has depended on a search for data pattern. Give the children plenty of practice in looking for pattern in their own results and those of their classmates. Do tell the children that the pattern we look for may demonstrate a positive *or* a negative *or* no link between variables, and all these patterns can be equally important.

Data interpretation, evaluation and explanation

This links closely to an understanding of data pattern. However, it may be set separately in the Programme of Study in order to draw our attention to the 'feedback' ideas in experimentation. When they have done an experiment children need to be able to say 'What do my results mean when I recall what it is I was trying to do?' This promotes judgements about the success of the experiment and how it could be modified. The National Curriculum Statutory Orders for Technology stress the importance of these kinds of skills. With judicious planning, and giving children individual and small-group problem-solving exercises, they should be able to carry some investigations beyond the 'one try and write it up' format of much junior science.

Experimental and investigative science

As explained in the introduction, all the skills required for this are developed through the activities in Life Processes and Living Things, Materials and their Properties and Physical Processes.

In order to enable you to identify the work on scientific investigations as the children work on the content of science in the above coverage of the Programme of Study for Experimental and Investigative Science, a set of symbols has been used. You will find these symbols at the end of appropriate activities to denote which skills are covered. They also appear on the accompanying copymasters. You can record children's experience of these skills on the Record Sheet at the back of the book.

The content of Experimental and Investigative Science at each level is summarised as follows:

Level descriptions: Experimental and investigative science

Level descriptions and 'best fits' with the Programme of study symbols

The following Level descriptions describe the types and range of performance that pupils working at a particular level should characteristically demonstrate. In deciding on a pupil's level of attainment at the end of a Key Stage, teachers should judge which description best fits the pupil's performance. Each description should be considered in conjunction with the descriptions for adjacent levels.

By the end of Key Stage 2, the performance of the great majority of pupils should be within the range 2 to 5.

Level 2

Pupils respond to suggestions of how to find things out and, with help, make their own suggestions. They use simple equipment provided and make observations related to their task. They compare objects, living things and events they observe. They describe their observations and record them using simple tables where it is appropriate to do so. They say whether what happened was what they expected.

Level 3

Pupils respond to suggestions, put forward their own ideas and, where appropriate, make simple predictions. They make relevant observations and measure quantities, such as length or mass, using a range of simple equipment. With some help they carry out a fair test, recognising and explaining why it is fair. They record their observations in a variety of ways. They provide explanations for observations and, where they occur, for simple patterns in recorded measurements. They say what they have found out from their work.

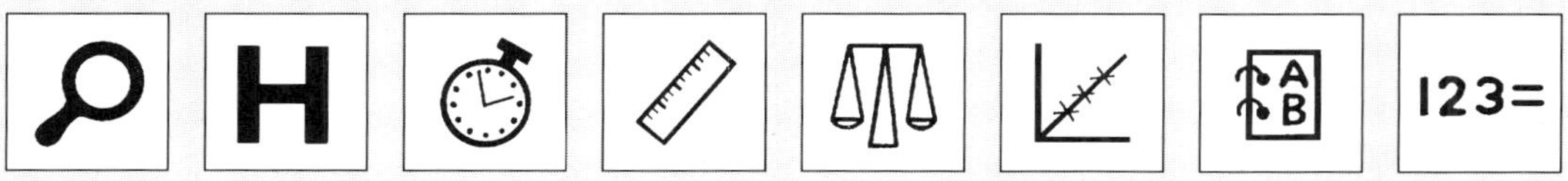

Level 4

Pupils recognise the need for fair tests, describing, or showing in the way they perform their task, how to vary one factor whilst keeping others the same. Where appropriate, they make predictions. They select suitable equipment to use and make a series of observations and measurements that are adequate for the task. They present their observations and measurements clearly, using tables and bar charts. They begin to plot points to form simple graphs and use these graphs to point out and interpret patterns or trends in their data. They take account of these patterns when they draw conclusions, and begin to relate their conclusions to scientific knowledge and understanding.

Level 5

Pupils identify the key factors they need to consider in contexts that involve only a few factors. Where appropriate, they make predictions based on their scientific knowledge and understanding. They select apparatus for a range of tasks and use it with care. They make a series of observations or measurements with precision appropriate to the task. They begin to repeat observations and measurements and to offer simple explanations for any differences they encounter. They record observations and measurements systematically and present data as line graphs. They draw conclusions that are consistent with the evidence and begin to relate these to scientific knowledge and understanding.

Life processes and living things

How the Areas of study in this book relate to the section of the Programme of study and Attainment target level descriptions.

Programme of study		Areas of study and 'best fit' with Level descriptions			
		Level description 2	**Level description 3**	**Level description 4**	**Level description 5**
1. Life processes	Pupils should be taught: **a** that there are life processes, including nutrition, movement, growth and reproduction, common to animals, including humans;	Areas of study: 1, 2	Areas of study: 4, 5, 6		
	b that there are life processes, including growth, nutrition and reproduction, common to plants.	Area of study: 3	Areas of study: 5, 6		
2. Humans as organisms **nutrition**	**a** the functions of teeth and the importance of dental care;	Area of study: 7	Area of study: 9		
	b that food is needed for activity and for growth, and that an adequate and varied diet is needed to keep healthy;	Area of study: 8	Area of study: 10		
circulation	**c** a simple model of the structure of the heart and how it acts as a pump;			Area of study: 11	Area of study: 12
	d how blood circulates in the body through arteries and veins;				Area of study: 12
	e the effect of exercise and rest on pulse rate;				Area of study: 13
movement	**f** that humans have skeletons and muscles to support their bodies and to help them to move;			Area of study: 14	
growth and reproduction	**g** the main stages of the human life cycle;	Area of study: 15		Area of study: 16	
health	**h** that tobacco, alcohol and other drugs can have harmful effects.			Area of study: 17	

Life processes and living things

How the Areas of study in this book relate to the section of the Programme of study and Attainment target level descriptions.			Areas of study and 'best fit' with Level descriptions			
Programme of study			**Level description 2**	**Level description 3**	**Level description 4**	**Level description 5**
3. Green plants as organisms		Pupils should be taught:				
growth and nutrition	**a**	that plant growth is affected by the availability of light and water, and by temperature;		Area of study: 18		
	b	that plants need light to produce food for growth, and the importance of the leaf in this process;			Area of study: 19	
	c	that the root anchors the plant, and that water and nutrients are taken in through the root and transported through the stem to other parts of the plant;			Area of study: 20	
reproduction	**d**	about the life cycle of flowering plants, including pollination, seed production, seed dispersal and germination.	Area of study: 21	Area of study: 22	Area of study: 23	Area of study: 24
4. Variation and classification	**a**	how locally occurring animals and plants can be identified and assigned to groups, using keys.	Area of study: 25		Area of study: 26	Areas of study: 27–31
5. Living things in their environment **adaptation**	**a**	that different plants and animals are found in different habitats;	Area of study: 32	Area of study: 33	Areas of study: 34, 35	
	b	how animals and plants in two different habitats are suited to their environment;			Areas of study: 34, 36	
feeding relationships	**c**	that food chains show feeding relationships in an ecosystem;			Area of study: 37	
	d	that nearly all food chains start with a green plant;			Area of study: 37	
micro-organisms	**e**	that micro-organisms exist, and that many may be beneficial, *e.g. in the breakdown of waste,* while others may be harmful, *e.g. in causing disease.*		Area of study: 38		Area of study: 39

Level descriptions: Life processes and living things

Level 2

Pupils use their knowledge about living things to describe basic conditions, such as a supply of food, water, air or light, that animals and plants need in order to survive. They recognise that living things grow and reproduce. They sort living things into groups, using simple features. They describe the basis for their groupings in terms such as number of legs or shape of leaf. They recognise that different living things are found in different places, such as ponds or woods.

Level 3

Pupils use their knowledge of basic life processes, such as growth or reproduction, when they describe differences between living and non-living things. They provide simple explanations for changes in living things, such as diet affecting the health of humans or other animals, or lack of light or water altering plant growth. They identify ways in which an animal is suited to its environment, such as a fish having fins to help it swim.

Level 4

Pupils demonstrate knowledge and understanding of aspects of Life processes and living things drawn from the Key Stage 2 or Key Stage 3 Programme of Study. They use scientific names for some major organs of body systems, such as the circulatory system, and identify the position of these organs in the human body. They identify organs, such as petal, stamen or stigma, of different plants they observe. They use keys based on observable external features to help them to identify and group living things systematically. They recognise that feeding relationships exist between plants and animals in a habitat, and describe these relationships using food chains and terms such as predator and prey.

Level 5

Pupils demonstrate an increasing knowledge and understanding of aspects of Life processes and living things drawn from the Key Stage 2 or Key Stage 3 Programme of Study. They describe the main functions of some organs of the human body, such as the heart, and of the flowering plant, such as the petal, stamen or stigma. They explain how these functions are essential to the organism. They describe the main stages of the life cycles of humans and flowering plants and point out similarities. They recognise that there is a great variety of living things and understand the importance of classification. They explain that different organisms are found in different habitats because of differences in environmental factors, such as the availability of light or water.

Programme of study: Life processes and living things

Work on life processes should be related to pupils' knowledge of animals and plants in the local environment. Work on the variety of life in a habitat should be linked to the reasons for classifying living things.

Pupils should be taught:

1. Life processes

a that there are life processes, including nutrition, movement, growth and reproduction, common to animals, including humans;

b that there are life processes, including growth, nutrition and reproduction, common to plants.

Area of study 1 | P of S 1a | LD 2

SUSTAINING HUMAN LIFE PROCESSES

C13

Purpose
To help the children examine what their basic needs are.

Materials needed
Dolls with doll-size furniture, clothes and crockery; or a doll's house or model farm.

Activity: Our needs
Discuss with the children what they think their needs are, using the dolls or the house/farm to demonstrate all the things we do every day to satisfy basic needs. The need for warmth, food and drink, air and sleep will come out of the discussion.

The children can then help set up a display of dolls to show life-sustaining needs. Or they could set up the doll's house/farm with dolls eating, sleeping, dressed in clothes and outside getting 'fresh air'.

You can explain to the children that we have other needs that may not be *essential* to life, but which are nonetheless very important. They include love and exercise.

Get the children to record in pictures their own needs on copymaster 13.

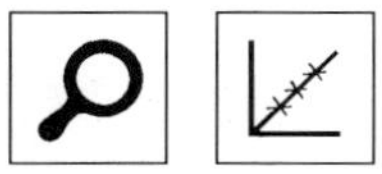

Area of study 2 | P of S 1a | LD 2

SUSTAINING ANIMALS' LIVES

Purpose
To learn how pets and other animals should be looked after.

Materials needed
A range of pets; beginners' books about pets.

Activity 1: Pets
Do a 'pet survey' among the children. Get the group of children with each pet to record how they care for their pets, and display as a mini-topic. Those children who do not have a pet can learn about the school pet if there is one, or work on a pet belonging to one of their friends.

Activity 2: Animal care
Invite someone to come and talk to the children about animal care. It could be a zookeeper, petshop owner or someone representing the RSPCA or RSPB. Alternatively, consult the local 'what's on' section in the paper or library to find out whether there is a local Natural History Group or Ornithological Society. Such a group may welcome the chance to tell children how to protect the habitat of wild creatures and how to observe them properly. If you do decide to invite a visitor, the visit does require some research on your part. If possible, meet the speaker, establish what he/she needs (e.g. projector, birdcage) and give him/her a brief. Tell him/her the context for the children's learning and the kind of thing you would like to be included in the talk, if possible. Try and persuade him/her to bring some slides (or preferably live creatures) for the children to see. Also ask if there are some things which he/she can bring that you may borrow for a while. For example, a bag of birdseed, a brush used for cleaning an elephant or even an unused dog kennel from the pet shop will contribute much more to the children's learning than any number of slides. You will also have the makings of an enthralling display.

Activity 3: Pet show
Have a pets' corner or pet show. You will need some parental help and the permission of the parents. Give the children a written note to say that they are allowed to bring their pet to school on the special day, providing it is in a container through which it can be seen and from which it cannot escape. Cover everywhere with newspaper and be prepared to spend the day being a zookeeper. The children who bring pets can be the experts on pet care. All the children can do some close observation and some drawing from life, and make comparisons of the needs of different pets. You may get the chance to compile a short quiz on the show, with questions such as: 'What do rabbits eat?', 'What does Monica give her hamster to play with?'; and tasks such as: 'Name one nocturnal pet', 'Name one pet which eats all kinds of food', etc.

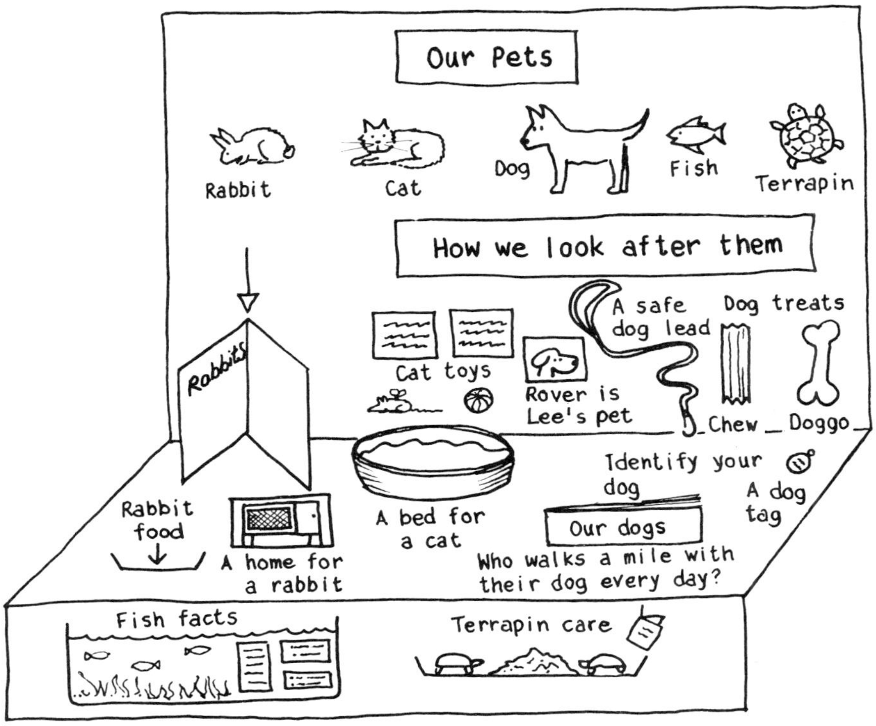

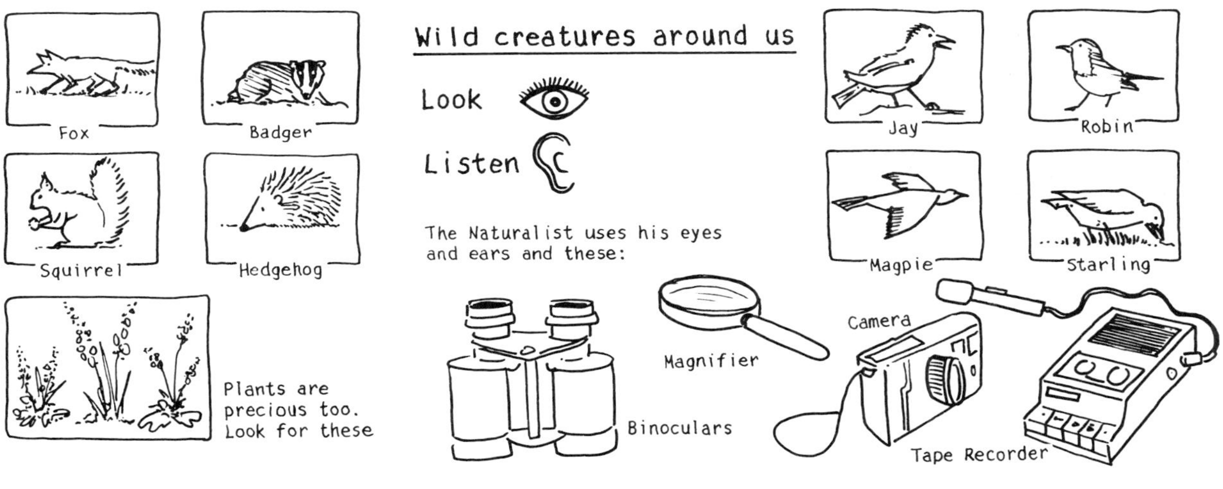

Area of study 3 | P of S 1b | LD 2

SUSTAINING PLANT LIFE PROCESSES

C14

Purpose
To show that plants can only thrive when their vital needs are met.

Materials needed
Seeds, small flowerpots, seed compost, small watering can or jug, sugar paper.

Activity: Plant needs
Help the children to decide what they think a plant needs to grow. Then help them test some of these ideas by growing grass, cress or broad beans under the following conditions:

Pot 1: soil, no water, light. Plant the seed. Do not water. Place in light.
Pot 2: soil, water, no light. Plant the seed. Water regularly but keep covered.
Pot 3: no soil, water, light. Put seed in empty pot. Water regularly and place in the light.
Pot 4: soil, water, light. Plant the seed. Water regularly and place in the light.

Pot 2 can be placed in the dark by making a cylinder out of sugar paper to enclose the pot, and fitting it with a lid. Depending on the kind of seed and other environmental conditions the seeds may all germinate, but the growth should be most vigorous where all the experimental needs are met, i.e. pot 4.

The children can record the results of the experiment on copymaster 14.

Area of study 4 | P of S 1a | LD 3

THE COMMONALITY OF LIFE PROCESSES

C15–16

Purpose
To show that feeding, breathing, support, movement and certain behaviours are common to humans and other animals.

Materials needed
Pictures of human beings and other animals, an animal skeleton and a model of a human skeleton, shells and fish bones, small live creatures to observe (for example, mini-beasts or school pets), information about the children's pets, books about the animal world, videos of wildlife and pet care programmes.

Activity 1: Feeding
Discuss the kinds of foods that we like to eat. Compare our diet with that of pets like cats and dogs, domestic animals like cows and hens and wild animals including, for example, elephants and lions. Using pictures of a variety of animals, let the children group them according to whether they eat plants (herbivores), meat (carnivores) or both (omnivores). Discuss the likely effects of an animal's diet on where it lives and how it behaves.

Talk about the effects on animals of a poor diet or insufficient food. Relate this discussion to animal migration and hibernation.

Activity 2: Breathing
Discuss the similarities in breathing between ourselves and other animals. Find out how other animal groups breathe.

Water is the source of oxygen for fish, and the oxygen is taken into their bodies through their gills. The water is sucked in through the mouth and expelled from the gills through the gill covers. Show the children some fish so that they can observe these movements.

Activity 3: Support
Look at an animal skeleton or animal bones or a model of the human skeleton, alongside the shells of creatures like snails and crabs, and the bones of a fish. Talk about how the skeletons of these creatures give support and some protection to their soft organs, as well as a frame on which to attach muscles.

Activity 4: Movement
Watch some wildlife videos and discuss the typical movements of animals in the wild. Look at some fish in water and birds in flight, in life where possible, but also on film or video. With the help of the children assemble all the kinds of words that we can use to describe the movements of fish, birds and other animals.

Ask the children to examine typical movements their pets make, and describe them or draw the movement sequence. Collate all the children's work in a class display.

Use a series of movement lessons to let the children explore the ways of moving typical of a variety of animals. These 'animal movement' routines could form a powerful addition to an assembly or a presentation to other classes.

Activity 5: 'Behaviour'
Discuss with the children the idea that some behaviours are instinctive and some are learned. Instinctive behaviour is common to all members of a species.

Discuss what we mean when we say 'good behaviour' or 'naughty behaviour' in humans; how we communicate with each other, the kinds of 'patterns' in what we do and when certain behaviours are appropriate (for example shaking hands, waving and clapping, having a cuddle). Discuss what non-verbal behaviour is and how, by gesture and expression we, like other animals, can let others know how we feel.

Collect anecdotes about the children's pets. You may need some exploratory questions to start the discussion. Here are some examples:

- What does your dog do when a stranger comes to the door? When he is hungry? When he wants a game?
- What does your hamster do when he first wakes up? When some new food or bedding arrives?

Watch a wildlife video or look at pictures of animals in the wild and talk about how they communicate, how animal 'mums' and 'dads' behave, and what animals do, for example, when sick, content, or frightened. You could add a study of hibernation or migration to the behaviour patterns the children look at.

Activity 6: Life processes
Bring together all the children's work from Activities 1–4 into a whole class consolidation exercise. Here are some examples:

- A dramatic presentation entitled 'The animal world'
- A puppet show about life processes
- The story of Noah with additional discussion about animals' universal requirements.

The children can record some of their observations and discoveries made in the activities on copymasters 15 and 16.

Area of study 5 | P of S 1a, b | LD 3

REPRODUCTION

C17, 18

Purpose
To show that living things reproduce themselves.

Materials needed
Fruits and seeds and parent plants, flowerpots and potting compost; pictures of animal and human families.

Activity 1: Seeds
Let the children carefully examine the seeds and parent plants. If there are trees in or near the school grounds the children can collect their fruits and do rubbings, drawings and observation of them. Cut open a fruit to expose the seed. Talk about what will happen if the seed is planted. Plant some seeds. Get the children to label and care for them. Discuss their growth and when they will be large enough to plant out.

The children can picture record on copymaster 17.

Activity 2: Families
Collect pictures of animal and human families, including photographs brought in by the children. Arrange a family picture exhibition or a large family album containing all these pictures. The children can learn some of the words we use in association with animal families, such as litter, bitch, dog and pups, female, male and offspring. Discuss with them the idea that succeeding generations are always of the same species, in both animals and plants.

Let the children complete copymaster 18 to consolidate this idea.

An album of families

Area of study 6 | P of S 1a, b | LD 3

DAYS AND SEASONS

C19, 20

Purpose
To demonstrate that all living creatures, including plants and animals, are affected by daily and seasonal changes.

Materials needed
Trees in the school grounds or within sight of the school; school pets or the children's own pets for observation; reference books on plants, birds and animals.

Activity 1: Daily lives of animals
For the children to start thinking about what changes take place over each 24-hour period in the lives of creatures, they could start with themselves.

They can record in pictures their main activities over one 24-hour period on copymaster 19. They can then record the 24-hour pattern for another creature on a second copy of the copymaster (e.g. a pet dog, or a 'wild' creature they have researched in the books, such as a mouse or robin). The illustration at the top of the next page is an example of the type of work the children may produce.

Results and discussion should reveal the effects of night and day (though humans cheat somewhat by lighting and heating their homes). The children could be helped to speculate on times past when we were more at the mercy of 'natural' light and temperatures.

Activity 2: A case study
This is quite a complex piece of research to do, and as it has to be done over a period of time, will depend on your encouragement and organisation. The task is to choose a tree or animal and look at the effect of seasonal changes on the thing you have chosen. If it is done by direct observation, which is probably the best way, then the children need to systematically record information in each of the four seasons of the year.

For example, they may choose a holly or oak tree in the school grounds. If there is no available living thing which they can observe directly, they can research an animal (e.g. swallow or hedgehog) and write about that. It may be best to let them do this work from secondary sources in four stages, so that they can 'feel' the seasons in turn as they write about them.

It is probably best if they complete a new copymaster 20 for each season.

A day in the life of Elaine Brooks (Lisa's mum)

7am	9am	10am	12 noon	2pm	4pm	6pm	8pm	10pm
Make tea Call children	School run Shop Cook lunch Take Norman to Tots	Go to work	Fetch Norman from Tots Feed Norman	Go to park Call on Mrs Bloggs	Fetch children Help with homework	Cook tea	Watch TV Ironing Letters	Bed

A day in the life of The Female Hirundo Rustica (Swallow)

5am	6am →	8pm
Clean nest	Feed babies	Sleep

Programme of study: Life processes and living things

2. Humans as organisms

Pupils should be taught:

nutrition

a the functions of teeth and the importance of dental care;

b that food is needed for activity and for growth, and that an adequate and varied diet is needed to keep healthy;

Area of study 7 | P of S 2a | LD 2

TEETH

Purpose
To explain what teeth are for and why we look after them.

Materials needed
Information about human teeth and dental health; a wash bag and contents; mirrors.

Activity 1: A look at teeth
Encourage the children to look at their own teeth in a mirror, and at their friends' teeth. Carry out teeth counts. Provide each child with a strip of red sugar paper, which they can cut in half to represent the upper and lower jaw. They can cut out white-paper teeth and glue them on to the jaws – making a model of their own mouth. To display the mouths, curve the pieces of paper that form the upper and lower jaws and attach the ends to a pin-board.

Ask the children to count and record how many teeth they have, how many they have lost, how many are milk teeth, how many are loose.

Activity 2: How to look after teeth
Using reliable dental information, show the children how teeth should be cleaned. Discuss how often we should clean them, and make a class chart of how frequently the children brush their teeth. Stress the importance of regular dental check-ups.

Area of study 8 | P of S 2b | LD 2

WHAT FOOD IS FOR

Purpose
To explain what the food groups are and why we eat them.

Materials needed
Empty food packaging from all the major food groups.

Activity: Food groups
Talk about the four main food groups: proteins, carbohydrates, fats and vitamins and minerals. Discuss what we should eat every day for health. Mention some of the foods which we should avoid or eat only occasionally. Ask the children to bring in the packaging for healthy foods belonging to the four groups, and display them.

Area of study 9 | P of S 2a | LD 3

DENTAL CARE

Purpose
To help the children to understand the need for dental care and visits to the dentist.

Materials needed
Information about dental health, including posters, toothpastes and toothbrush advertisements.

Activity 1: Action for healthy teeth
Ask the school dentist or nurse if they will pay a visit to the class to discuss dental health. With the children, decide on a number of points to put in an action plan. Display the outcomes along with dental care information (see below).

Activity 2: Dental care posters
Ask the children to draw a poster showing a healthy smile.

Area of study 10 | P of S 2b | LD 3

FOOD AND HEALTH

C21

Purpose
To explain that the body can be kept healthy by eating sufficient food as part of a balanced diet. To raise awareness of the effects of malnutrition.

Materials needed
Diet and health information (may be available from the school doctor); information about malnutrition from worldwide charitable organisations.

Activity 1: Components of a healthy diet
Remind the children of the four main food groups, and what to include in their daily food intake. Discuss the avoidance of too much sugar, fats and additives. They can devise a day's menu, to include foods they like and which are good for them.

Copymaster 21 provides a menu headings list.

Activity 2: Find out about malnutrition
Look at available literature on inadequate diet and malnutrition. Discuss the fact that although in Britain the majority of us may all eat enough, we also need to eat a balance of the right things.

Programme of study: Life processes and living things

2. Humans as organisms

Pupils should be taught:

circulation

- **c** a simple model of the structure of the heart and how it acts as a pump;
- **d** how blood circulates in the body through arteries and veins;
- **e** the effect of exercise and rest on pulse rate.

Area of study 11 | P of S 2c | LD 4

THE HEART AND OTHER ORGANS

C22

Purpose
To learn where major organs are in the body, including the heart.

Materials needed
Books, diagrams and models depicting the major organs in the body.

Activity: Organs in us
Show the children pictures, diagrams and models to identify the location of the major organs in the body: for example the heart, lungs, stomach, intestine, kidneys, reproductive organs and brain. Quiz the children to ensure they can point to the location of their own organs with reasonable accuracy.

Let the children complete some simple diagrams to show the location of these major organs.

Copymaster 22 is a body outline with some pictures of organs alongside. The children can draw arrows to the locations, or cut the drawings of organs out and stick them where they should go on the outline.

Area of study 12 | P of S 2c, d | LD 5

THE CIRCULATORY SYSTEM

Purpose
To learn the names and functions of parts of the circulatory system.

Materials needed
Books and charts about the circulatory system.

Activity 1: Circulation
Show the children pictures and diagrams of our circulatory system. In discussion raise at least the following points:

- The blood system is a travel system in the body; it collects and takes food and oxygen to the organs.
- The heart is a pump which drives the system.
- The heart pumps blood to and from the lungs to get oxygen, and to and from all the parts of the body to supply oxygen and other nutrients.
- Blood vessels are called arteries and veins; name some of the principal ones.
- Some veins are nearer the body surface than arteries, and the body temperature is regulated by some heat loss from these.
- Oxygen makes arterial blood lighter in colour than venous blood.
- Venous blood can flow less copiously than arterial blood because it has travelled far from the 'push' it received from the heart pump.

Let the children reproduce a diagram of the heart and major blood vessels.

Activity 2: Respiration and circulation
Find out what the children know about respiration. Make sure they understand that we need oxygen from the air to live, and that it is taken into our bodies via the blood stream from our lungs. Each time we take a breath we refill our lungs with air from which some of the oxygen is then taken up. When we do strenuous exercise like running, we breathe faster to pull more oxygen supplies into our bodies.

Let the children copy a drawing or diagram of our respiratory system.

Discuss the process by which de-oxygenated blood is pumped to the lungs by the heart, and returned to the heart when oxygenated to be pumped around the body.

Area of study 13 | P of S 2e | LD 5

PULSE RATE

Purpose
To look at the effects of exercise and rest on pulse rate.

Materials needed
Reference books about health and fitness; a timer or watch with a minute hand.

Activity 1: Exercise, fitness and pulse rate
Talk to the children about what they think exercise is, and what it does. Let them measure their own pulse rate before exercise, by holding the inside of their wrist with two fingers while applying pressure on the back of the wrist with the thumb. They will need a timer or watch with a second hand. If they time their pulse for 30 seconds they can work out the rate per minute. Then ask them to run on the spot for a couple of minutes before retaking their pulse rate. The ensuing discussion may help them to understand the role of exercise in keeping the circulatory and respiratory systems working well, and that exercise can therefore help to prevent the onset of circulatory disorders.

Activity 2: Rest and pulse rate
Invite the children to measure their own pulse rate before they get out of bed in the morning, and then again when they arrive at school. Compare the results.

Programme of study: Life processes and living things

2. Humans as organisms

Pupils should be taught:

movement

f that humans have skeletons and muscles to support their bodies and to help them to move.

Area of study 14 | P of S 2f | LD 4

THE HUMAN SKELETON AND MUSCLES

Purpose
To find out the names of parts of the skeleton, and the functions of the skeleton and muscles.

Materials needed
A model skeleton (anatomically correct) or a specimen skeleton; charts showing muscle systems and how a muscle works.

Activity 1: Skeleton parts
Help the children to name the bones in the human body. Write these on to a diagram and ask the children to label a drawing of their own in the same way.

Point out how parts of the skeleton **support** and **protect** (for example the rib cage protects the heart and lungs).

Activity 2: Muscles
Use a chart to show how muscles are attached to bones, and explain that it is muscles that enable us to move.

Let the children feel their own muscles when tense (and working) and when relaxed.

Programme of study: Life processes and living things

2. Humans as organisms

Pupils should be taught:

growth and reproduction

g the main stages of the human life cycle.

Area of study 15 | P of S 2g | LD 2

THE HUMAN LIFE CYCLE

Purpose
To show what the stages are in a human's life.

Materials needed
Pictures of people, young and old, from magazines; photos brought in by the children of members of their own families.

Activity: Ages and stages
Discuss ages and stages with the children. Let them order some pictures according to age and stage. Look at generations in their own families with them. Arrange a display of ages and stages using photographs and magazine pictures.

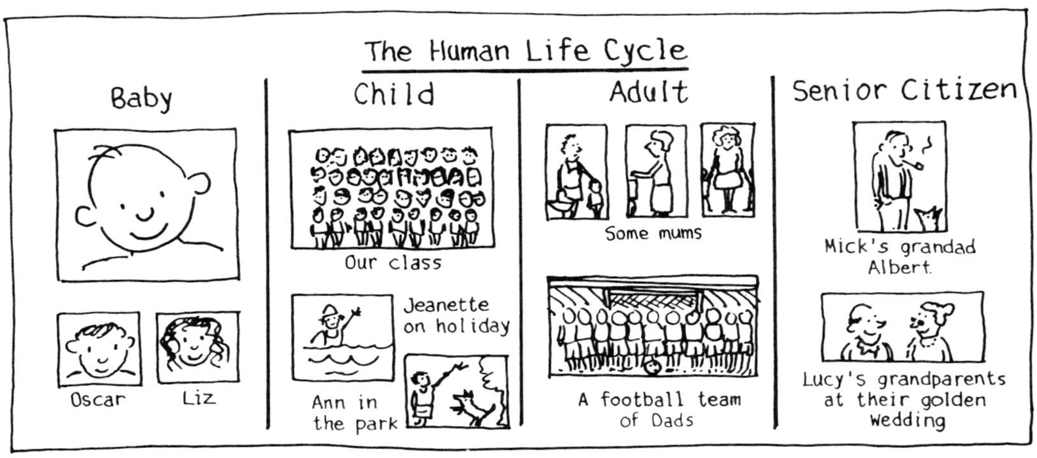

Area of study 16 | P of S 2g | LD 4

REPRODUCTION

C23

Purpose
To learn about the human reproductive system.

Materials needed
Illustrations showing male and female reproductive organs.

Activity: Reproduction
Let parents know before you undertake this activity. Tell the children the names of the reproductive organs in the human male and female and the main steps in reproduction. Include fertilisation, the growth of the foetus and some information about pregnancy and birth.

Copymaster 23 shows diagrams of the male and female reproductive systems.

Programme of study: Life processes and living things

2. Humans as organisms

health

Pupils should be taught:

h that tobacco, alcohol and other drugs can have harmful effects.

Area of study 17 | P of S 2h | LD 4

EFFECTS OF DRUGS

Purpose
To discuss the effects of tobacco, alcohol and other drugs.

Materials needed
Information about tobacco, alcohol, and other drugs, including solvents.

Activity 1: Effects of tobacco and alcohol and other drugs
This is an area that needs careful handling. Find out the statistics about health and drug-taking, and give the children the plain facts. They will all know people, probably in their own family, who smoke and drink, so if you reveal strong opinions you may upset some families. Children do need to know however, at this age, the risks from activities such as smoking, drinking and sniffing glue.

Activity 2: Healthy life plans
Using appropriate literature about drugs, (including nicotine and alcohol) ask the children firstly to write a list of dos and don'ts for a healthy life, and secondly to write some advertising material for any 'anti' campaign of their choice.

Programme of study: Life processes and living things

3. Green plants as organisms

growth and nutrition

Pupils should be taught:

a that plant growth is affected by the availability of light and water, and by temperature;

b that plants need light to produce food for growth, and the importance of the leaf in this process;

c that the root anchors the plant, and that water and nutrients are taken in through the root and transported through the stem to other parts of the plant.

Area of study 18 | P of S 3a | LD 3

PLANT GROWTH

C24–26

Purpose
To show that plant growth is affected by the availability of light, water and temperature.

Materials needed
Seeds, small flowerpots, seed compost, a small watering can or jug, sugar paper, a calibrated jug, a propagator.

Activity 1: Plant needs
This experiment is similar to that in the activity in Area of study 3. This time set up three pots with seeds, in the following conditions:

Pot 1: soil, no water, light. Plant the seed. Do not water. Place in light.

Pot 2: soil, water, no light. Plant the seed. Water regularly but keep covered.

Pot 3: soil, water, light. Plant the seed. Water regularly and place in the light.

Pot 2 can be placed in the dark by making a cylinder out of sugar paper to enclose the pot, and fitting it with a lid. All the pots should be placed in a warm area.

Place three similar pots in a cold area. Label them: 1 cold, 2 cold and 3 cold.

Depending on the kind of seed and other environmental conditions the seeds may all germinate, but the growth should be most vigorous where all the experimental needs are met, i.e. pot 3 (warm).

The children can record the results of the experiment on copymaster 24.

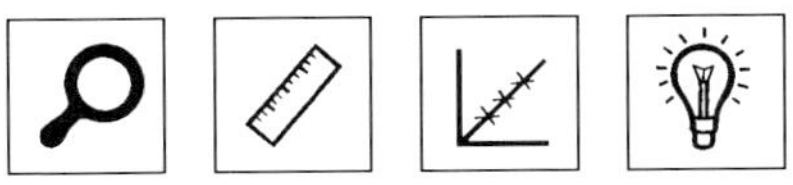

Activity 2: Varying the amount of light
Try planting up three pots with seeds and put one on the windowsill in full light, one in a shady place and one in the stock cupboard, or conditions of almost total darkness. Ask the children to water the pots at regular intervals with similar volumes of water, but otherwise leave them undisturbed.

Results should show that in all pots the seedlings lean towards any light source available. The pot in the shade can be turned around once the seedlings have started to lean towards the light, and they should, given time, lean the other way.

Copymaster 25 is a record sheet for this experiment.

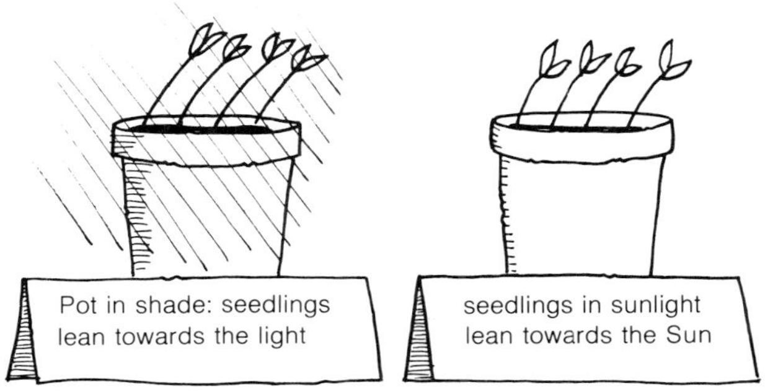

Activity 3: Varying the amount of water
Plant up three pots with similar quantities of compost or earth and put some seeds in them. Leave the pots side by side in the light. Let the children water two of the pots at intervals, giving one pot enough water to leave the compost thoroughly moist and the other so much water that the seedlings are permanently water-logged. Leave the third pot entirely without water. Let the children record what happens, and draw conclusions. If the seeds you plant are water-tolerant they will thrive no matter how much water the children give them. Absence of water should inhibit growth markedly.

Copymaster 26 allows the children to record the experiment formally.

Activity 4: Varying the temperature
If possible, find two locations in school which contrast in temperature at all times, but where the light levels and amount of moisture in the air are likely to be similar. (Sensors would be very useful in establishing the optimum places in school which meet these criteria.) Plant up two pots with similar compost and seeds and place one in each location. Give them similar quantities of water. After some growing time, it should be possible to see that heat helps growth (providing the seedlings are not exposed to too high a temperature).

Have a look at a commercial propagator, or make one using a vivarium or plastic box which can be covered with plastic sheeting. Discuss why these are used to 'bring on' germination or promote early growth. (If the children monitor the temperature inside and outside the propagator they should detect the temperature difference.) Seeds can be grown in the propagator to prove the point, but remember to tell the children that the water vapour inside a closed propagator is confined, creating an atmosphere which is not only warm but also damp.

Area of study 19 | P of S 3b | LD 4

WHY PLANTS NEED LIGHT

Purpose
To explain that plants need light to make food.

Materials needed
A picture of a potato plant showing leaves, stems, roots; potatoes or a freshly-dug potato plant; iodine and a dropper.

Activity 1: To discuss plants' need for light
Remind the children of work they may have completed in Area of Study 18, Activities 1 and 2, or replicate these experiments. Then, tell the children that the leaves lean towards light because they use energy from sunlight to make food. The food is glucose, a sugar. The plant converts this into starch. In a potato plant, the food or starch is stored in **tubers** underground – potatoes.

Iodine changes colour from orange to dark blue when it touches starch. Drop iodine on to the cut surface of a potato. The iodine turns blue.

Area of study 20 | P of S 3c | LD 4

WHY PLANTS HAVE ROOTS

Purpose
To explain that roots are vital to plant life.

Materials needed
Three seedlings – choose some that germinate quickly and have good thick root systems, like beans; liquid plant food, food colouring, water, three glass jars to place seedlings in.

Activity 1: To show that roots absorb water and other things if in solution
Fill the jars with clear water, coloured water and dilute liquid plant food respectively. Then, place a seedling in each jar.

After a few days the roots of the seedlings should have grown, those in coloured water and plant food should take on the colour of these solutions. Explain that the roots have absorbed water and things dissolved in the water. This is how plants obtain water and nutrients from the soil.

Ask the children to predict what would happen if the roots were removed. Cut the roots off a seedling. Place it in a jar alongside the first set of seedlings, and leave for several days. The children can observe whether it survives or not.

Programme of study: Life processes and living things

3. Green plants as organisms

Pupils should be taught:

reproduction

d about the life cycle of flowering plants, including pollination, seed production, seed dispersal and germination.

Area of study 21 | P of S 3d | LD 2

PLANT AND GROW

Purpose
To introduce the children to the idea that plants have a life cycle.

Materials needed
A variety of bulbs, seeds and plants; growing medium, pots, garden trowels, labels; pictures of seeds, seedlings, flowers and fruit.

Activity 1: Growing plants
Using a part of the school garden, pots and tubs or individual flower pots, allow the children to grow a variety of plants. Some could be planted as seeds or bulbs, and observed until they seed or flower. Others could be inspected for signs of general growth. Encourage the children to examine the plants very carefully, describe what they see, use magnifiers and sketch important features.

Activity 2: Plant life cycle
Help children to sequence pictures of plant life cycles.

Area of study 22 | P of S 3d | LD 3

SEED DISPERSAL

Purpose
To study seed dispersal.

Materials needed
A variety of fruits and seeds, for example beech, acorn, ash, sycamore, burr, cone, dandelion, cherry, tomato; magnifiers.

Activity 1: Types of seed and fruit
Encourage the children to examine a variety of fruits and seeds using magnifiers, and to draw them. If possible, the children can search for fruits and seeds in a field or park.

Draw on the children's descriptions to compile banks of words which could be used to resource further work about fruits and seeds.

Activity 2: Dispersal
Explore with the children the part played by wind, water and animals (eating and carrying seeds) during the process of seed dispersal.

Area of study 23 | P of S 3d | LD 4

MAJOR ORGANS IN PLANTS

C27

Purpose
To identify and name the organs of flowering plants.

Materials needed
Specimen flowering plants, with flowers that can be sliced through for examination; craft knife, magnifiers, charts and books about flowering plants.

Activity: Organs in flowering plants
Encourage the children to examine the flowering plants. These could be sliced in half and viewed through magnifiers. Plants having large single flower heads may prove easier for the children to work on, for example daffodils, tulips, daisies and dandelions. The children could draw what they see and research the names of the plant organs.

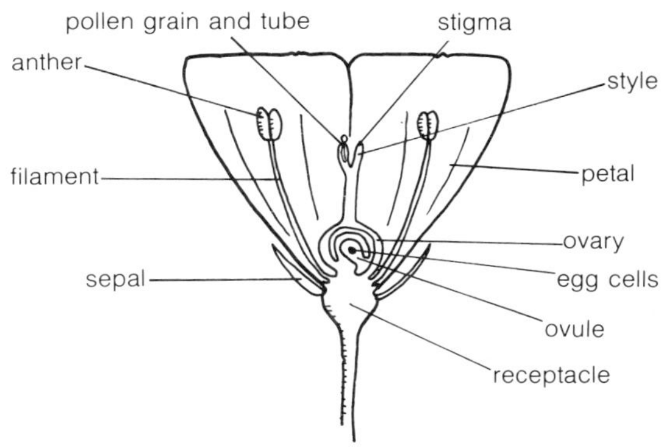

Copymaster 27 is a drawing of a flowering plant ready for labelling.

Area of study 24 | P of S 3b,c,d | LD 5

ORGAN SYSTEMS IN PLANTS

Purpose
To identify and learn the functions of the major organ systems in flowering plants.

Materials needed
Books and pictures about plants; specimens of flowering plants, including sections of them; magnifiers; celery or a carnation, a vessel of water and food colouring; seeds of flowering plants, for example sunflowers or marrows, some snowdrop or daffodil bulbs; a growing medium and pots.

Activity 1: Organ systems
Show the children how to draw flowering plants, from direct observation and using magnifiers. Use some of their detailed drawings and the specimens available to help them to identify the major organ systems. Consult library resources and botanical charts to ensure appropriate labelling.

Activity 2: Organ functions: Photosynthesis
Using carbon dioxide, sunshine and water, green plants produce food molecules. Chlorophyll enables the energy in sunlight to be used to split water molecules. Oxygen is given off. This is called the light reaction. The hydrogen from the water is then used to convert carbon dioxide into carbohydrates (food). This reaction is called 'dark' because it does not require sunlight. Let the children find out how this happens and which parts of the plant are necessarily involved.

Activity 3: Organ functions: Circulation
To demonstrate that water is taken up by a plant, put a stick of celery or a white carnation into water with a

little red food colouring in it, and leave it standing in the coloured water. After a while both celery and flower will have turned pink.

Activity 4: Organ functions: Reproduction
Encourage the children to plant the seeds and bulbs at the appropriate time of year, either in pots or in the school garden.

a) Seeds
- Follow seed packet instructions on planting and propagation.
- Observe growth and development through the production of flowers and fruits.
- When the fruits should ripen, remove seeds and keep them in dry conditions for planting the following year.

b) Bulbs
- Measure the circumference of the bulbs before planting.
- Plant in bulb fibre or other suitable medium, or if they are planted in the ground, make sure the soil is light around each bulb.
- Observe growth and development through the production of flowers.
- Leave the bulb plants until the foliage has died away and then examine them for size increase, indicating vegetative reproduction.
- If your class is a year group class of Y6, individual children may not be able to see through the whole activity, to the replanting of seeds. It is important that they are able to see the process through, and you may consider sending them a newsletter telling them of the growth patterns of seeds they grew, or taking specimens of a subsequent generation of plants along to their secondary school to show them.

Activity 5: Seed dispersal
The children may already have begun work on this subject area as part of Area of study 22, Activity 2. It provides a well-documented and discrete topic that an individual child or children may like to carry through. Using all their research skills, school resources and field work, they can investigate the methods of seed dispersal, including, for example, wind, explosive pods, birds eating them, being carried in the fur of animals, or by streams.

Programme of study: Life processes and living things

4. Variation and classification

Pupils should be taught:

a how locally occurring animals and plants can be identified and assigned to groups, using keys.

Area of study 25 | P of S 4a | LD 2

CHARACTERISTICS OF LIVING THINGS

C28, 29

Purpose
To begin to group living creatures according to their characteristics.

Materials needed
Mini-beasts (e.g. spiders, woodlice, caterpillars) and other available animals; bug-bottles and containers to collect animals in, and magnifiers, where necessary, to view them.

Activity 1: Animal varieties
Look carefully at a number of living creatures with the children. If you have school pets such as a budgie or fish, use them. If there are no school pets, collect mini-beasts. Remember where they were found so that they can be returned. Lift a stone where the soil is damp, shake a bush (having first spread newspaper or a plastic sheet beneath it), upturn a pile of leaves and there should be beetles, ladybirds, woodlice, snails, earthworms and more. Put them into see-through lidded pots. Make sure they are displayed where they are well-lit (but not left to dry out or overheat). Supply magnifiers and some clues as to what to look for to find similarities and differences.

Activity 2: Vertebrates and invertebrates
Construct a wormery. Set it up alongside some woodlice and a display of shells of animals such as cockles, crabs and winkles, and also some creatures with an internal skeleton (e.g. a fish).

The children can try a comparison and record their observations on copymaster 28.

Activity 3: Comparing other creatures with ourselves
Ask the children to do a systematic comparison between a mini-beast or fish and themselves. They will need to have the mini-beast/fish to look at. (If you cannot provide a live fish, a mackerel or herring from the fishmonger will do.)

Some possible criteria for comparison appear on copymaster 29.

Activity 4: A visit
Visit a zoo, bird sanctuary, aquarium or garden centre with the children, so that they can make some comparisons between different kinds of living things. You will need to research the kinds of creatures or plants you are going to see beforehand, and give the children clues about what to look for.

Area of study 26 | P of S 4a | LD 4

GROUPING LIVING THINGS

C30

Purpose
To show that creatures can be put into groups, and show how they may be grouped, using keys.

Materials needed
A selection of plants, for example flowering grasses or plants 'borrowed' from a garden centre, or a selection of mini-beasts; a computer, database software and reference books about the whole animal and plant world.

Activity 1: Similarities and differences
The children need to observe closely and compare a range of plants or mini-beasts to find out similarities and differences. Then they can start to assemble the trails in a sort of treasure hunt. For example, a simple key, for a collection of snails, slugs, earthworms, beetles, woodlice and millipedes may run like the flowchart below.

The key can then be developed further to identify different kinds of beetle, for example. Each time the children think they have the next distinguishing feature in the trail, they can put it to the test with one of their specimens and see if it works. You should relate this work to that on decision-making trees in Mathematics.

Once the children have developed their own 'keys' they should be shown some of the standard ones available. They should also have the chance to look at books about animals to discover the ways in which these are commonly grouped.

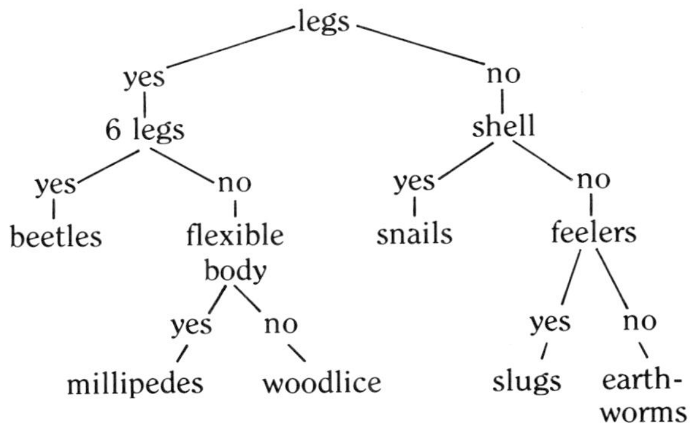

Activity 2: Creating a database about mammals
This activity involves accessing information on the computer and so is best done with children in groups of only two or three. Firstly the children need to research their information. In order to make the information manageable, let them choose five mammals for study. In rough they should write down a description of the important features and habits of each animal. Then they can find labels for things they have looked at in all the creatures, e.g. covering: fur or hair. Their database will start with labels such as these:

- Database: Mammals
- Name of animal
- Size in cm
- Covering
- Live babies/eggs
- How many young at a time
- Blood (warm/cold)

When their database is complete, they can print out all their information and store their data on disk. The next group of children can do the same task. When several groups of children have had a go they can compare their databases and see if they can be amalgamated (with your help). Then the computer will have sufficient entries for the children to access their database and print out sub-groups of animals, e.g. those mammals which commonly have more than three babies at a time.

Copymaster 30 will remind them of some of the details on their database.

Activity 3: Choosing and creating a database
Ask the children to construct a sophisticated database on the computer. They can devise it themselves, for at least 20 living creatures. They can then access that database and do sorts according to characteristics.

They can compare their own key with available published keys.

Activity 4: Creature quiz
Ask the children to compile a quiz on animal characteristics, using the information they collected for their own database. They can then test their classmates.

Area of study 27 | P of S 4a | LD 5

PEOPLE ARE ALIKE BUT DIFFER

C31

Purpose
To appreciate that some differences between human beings can be easily measured, and to measure some of them.

Materials needed
Sticky shapes, large sheets of paper to make charts, felt-tip markers, pencils, small slips of paper, coloured sugar paper.

Activity 1: Comparing foot sizes
Ask the children to draw round their right foot on coloured sugar paper and then to cut out the shape and write their name on it. They may find it easier to work in pairs, drawing round each other's feet. On a long strip of paper, e.g. wallpaper or lining paper, draw a base-line. Get the children to lay their cut-outs down so that the 'heel' is touching the base-line (see below). The shapes can be set in order by a child or several children while the rest look on. Start with the smallest, leading up to the biggest. Put the chart on display.

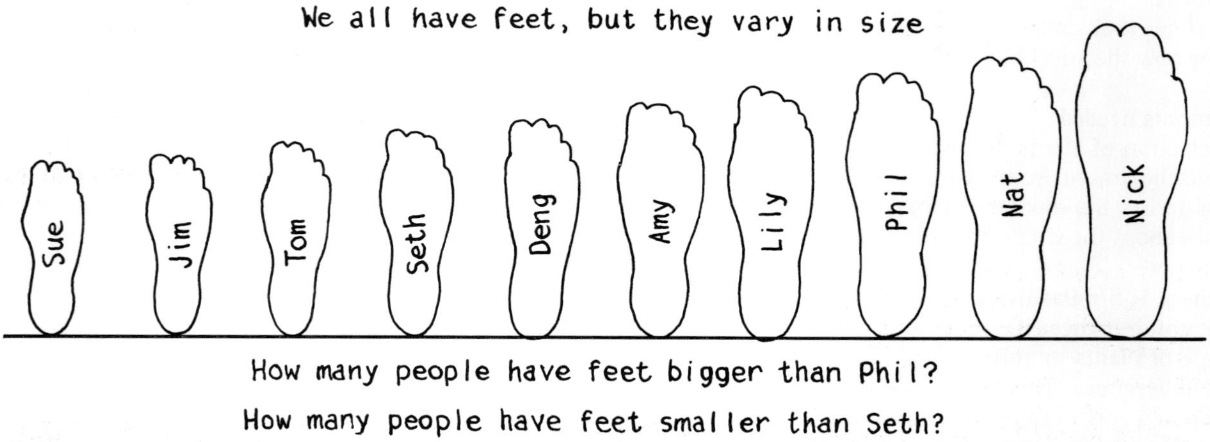

Activity 2: Comparing height
Fix a strip of paper to the wall or door frame so that the bottom edge just touches the floor. Get each child in turn to stand in their stocking-feet against the strip. Place a stiff piece of card flat on each one's head so that it touches the wall. Make a mark on the strip where the card touches. Then let them step away and write their name by the mark.

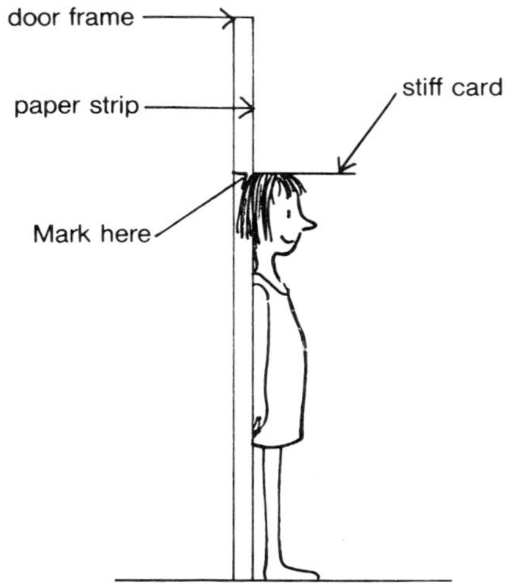

When all the children have a mark on the strip, take a metre rule and mark its height. Discuss with the children whether they are 'much taller' or 'a bit taller' then one metre. Let them decide whether a metre is a good unit to measure height, or whether we need to have some unit smaller than a metre to measure with. Display the results. If the same children have already done Activity 1 you can look for an association between the data, e.g. people with bigger feet may be taller. There will be opportunities here to talk about similarities in families, e.g. height, hair colour, eye colour, etc. of brothers, sisters, parents and grandparents.

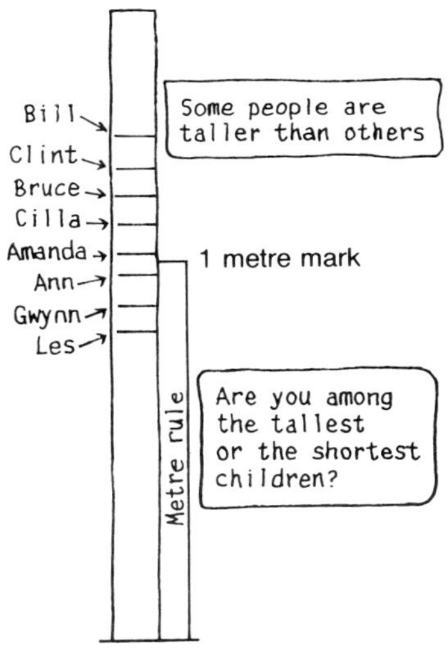

Activity 3: Comparing handspans
Lay a piece of paper flat on the table and draw a 'start line' down the left-hand side. Ask one child to do the recording. Get each child in turn to place their outstretched hand on the chart, with the starter finger or thumb just touching the 'start line'.

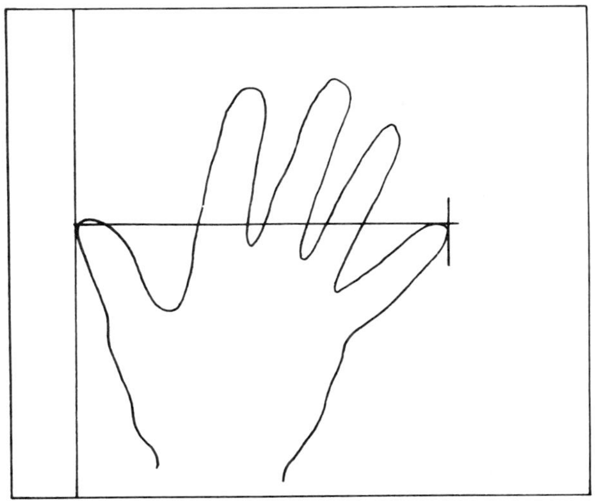

Lay hand on paper in outstretched position and mark beside little finger.

The extent of their handspan can be marked with a pencil, and later marked permanently with a felt tip or sticky paper strip. Put the chart on display.

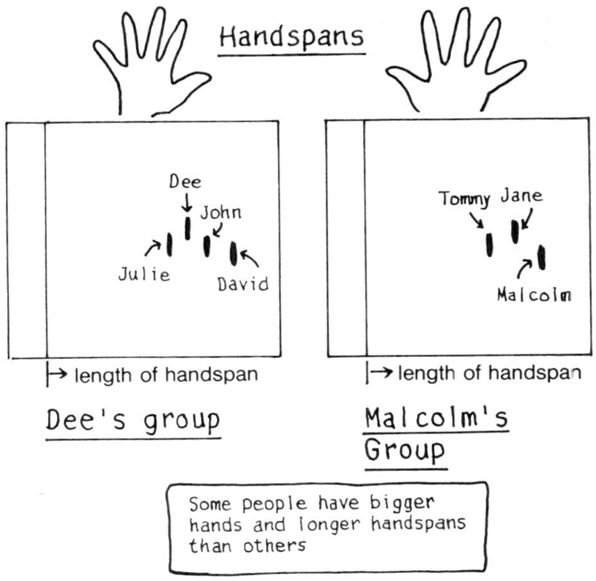

Copymaster 31 can be used for the children to make a footsize, height and handspan comparison between themselves and several of their friends.

Area of study 28 | P of S 4a | LD 5

FAMILY LIKENESS

C32

Purpose
To identify similarities between people in the same family.

Materials needed
Photographs brought in by the children of themselves and members of their families.

Activity 1: Look-alikes in the family
Remind the children of the work they completed for the activity in Area of study 15. The children can sift through the photographs for likenesses between members of their families. These can be placed on display for all to see, alongside an 'identikit' of clues to look for. They may be able to note, e.g. that most children of dark-haired parents have dark hair, and that sometimes children look more like their grandparents than their parents.

Activity 2: Personality likenesses in the family
The children should discuss the idea at home and report back. For example, Cleo may say that her mum says she has her dad's temper, her auntie's friendly ways and her grandad's brains. Help them to look at a wide range of personality characteristics, but do not let them take this analysis too seriously.

Activity 3: Family habits and mannerisms
The children will need to discuss this at home. It does seem to be the case that even things we do not think can be passed on from one person to another, such as chewing the lip or tweaking the thumbs, do sometimes recur in families. Again, this should be fairly light-hearted, as it has not yet been established exactly what is transmitted from one generation to the next.

The children can do a survey among family members, if you first ask their parents' permission. They can devise the questions they would like to ask, and collate them afterwards.

They can use copymaster 32 to collect information.

Activity 4: Genes
Tell the children that family likenesses are the result of the passing on of characteristics from one generation to the next. The information is carried by genes in the sperm and egg. There is an opportunity here to do work on codes and ciphers.

Area of study 29 | P of S 4a | LD 5

VARIATION IN THE SAME SPECIES

C33, 34

Purpose
To establish that animals of the same species vary one from another.

Materials needed
Some pets, either school pets or ones belonging to the children (several of each species); tape measures, large scales or weighing machine, magnifiers, pencils and paper.

Activity 1: Animal comparisons
Look carefully at the two or more examples of a species, e.g. perhaps you could borrow three pet rabbits, in separate cages. Ask the children to list as many features of the appearance as they can, e.g. fur colour, length of whiskers, appearance of fur. Then under each heading they can describe and compare the rabbits they are looking at in relation to these features. They can then talk to the rabbits' owners and ask about features they cannot see such as preferred diet and sleeping habits.

Using copymaster 33 the children can rule a column for each pet examined and compare across the columns the characteristics for each pet (e.g. fur colour, length of ears).

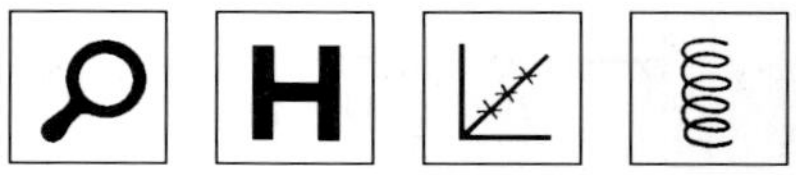

Activity 2: Measuring animal comparisons
When they have completed Activity 1, the children can try to detect and measure more detailed differences, e.g. stray hairs can be measured and their length compared; if the parentage of the animals is known, that can also be compared. They can, with the owners' help, weigh each animal and also weigh the amount of food it will eat in a day. They can record and compare all these results in tabular form and comment on how much difference there is between the sample animals of the same species.

Copymaster 34 can be used to tabulate this information.

Activity 3: Comparing many animals of the same species
Collect together as much information as you can about the varieties within a species. A straightforward example might be to look at domestic dogs or cats.

Area of study 30 | P of S 4a | LD 5

VARIATION WITHIN A PLANT FAMILY

Purpose
To identify that plant families vary just as animal families do.

Materials needed
Books about plant classification and plant families; packets of seeds including two or three varieties of the same flowering plant.

Activity 1: Comparing growth in plants of the same family
Plant seeds of two or three varieties of the same flowering plant. Get the children to monitor germination time, speed of growth of the shoot, how the first leaves emerge. They can record this information, and transfer it to a class chart (see below).

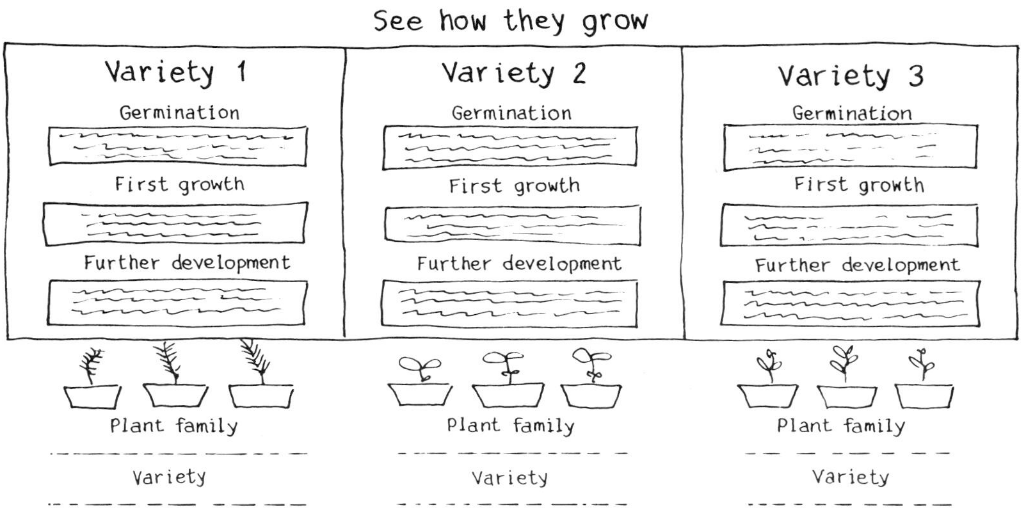

Activity 2: Comparing flowers in plants of the same family
Using the plants grown for Activity 1, or using plants that have been grown in the school greenhouse or bought in from a garden centre, get the children to observe closely, draw, cut in section and describe the flowers. They can record their results in tabular form.

Area of study 31 | P of S 4a | LD 5

VARIATIONS IN VEGETABLE VARIETIES

Purpose
To show that there is a wide range of variation within vegetable species.

Materials needed
Three kinds of outdoor tomato plants, named and labelled, and three kinds of french bean seed/plant or a similar vegetable; a caretaker gardener, or perhaps a parent who is a gardening enthusiast and who will keep an eye on the plants when the children are not there; growing bags or fertile garden plot, trowels and a watering can.

Activity 1: Comparing vegetables
Though the children can compare growth in the different plants, and will need to care for and stake them, the most important comparisons are to be made with the ripe vegetables. They can be observed, felt, weighed and (in the case of tomatoes) tasted. They can also be cut open to see if there are differences in colouring, shape and number of seeds inside. Again, results can be tabulated. When they begin to ripen, one of the plants can be lifted and planted in a large pot to add to a class display.

Programme of study: Life processes and living things

5. Living things in their environment

Pupils should be taught:

adaptation

a that different plants and animals are found in different habitats;

b how animals and plants in two different habitats are suited to their environment;

Area of study 32 | P of S 5a | LD 2

EXPLORING HABITATS

Purpose
To look for animals and plants in a variety of habitats.

Materials needed
Magnifiers, collecting jars and bags.

Activity 1: The school garden
If your school has a garden, playing field or even a grass verge at the front, let the children explore it to see what they can find in the way of animals that live there, and uncultivated plants that grow there. They may note some of the following:

- What the soil looks like
- Underlying rock (if visible or known)
- Plants and trees (draw and name some of them)
- Birds
- Small creatures like beetles and worms
- Signs of larger animals (droppings or holes)
- Low-growing plants if the grass is cut
- Where it is shady and where in full sun
- Where it is damp and where dry.

The school garden

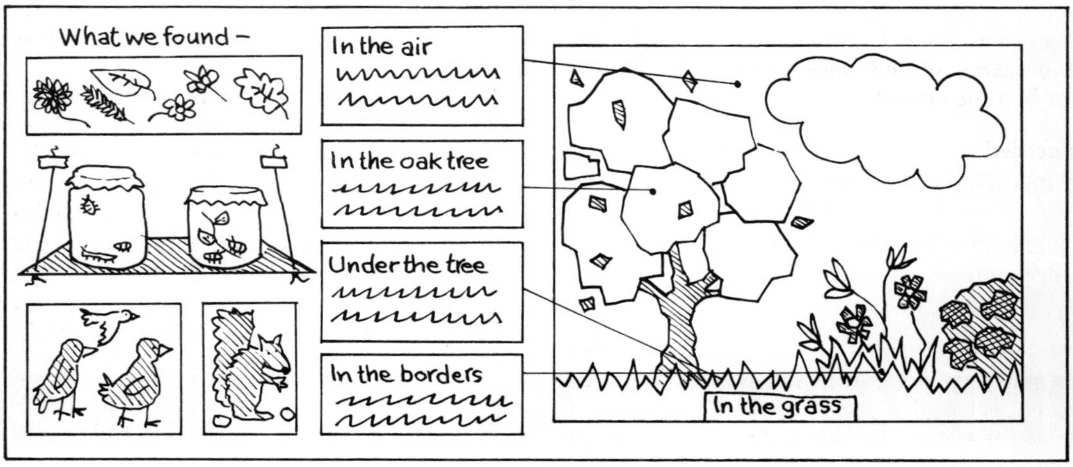

The children's findings can be recorded by you at the time using a tape recorder, or you can return to the classroom for a feedback discussion. If you and the children bring sample creatures into the classroom, remember to return them to the spot where found, after you have had a good look at them. Ask the children to produce either a single picture with about four of the things they saw on it, or small pictures which can be added to a collaborative collage. Names and labels can then be added by you.

It may be that yours is an inner-city school with only a tarmac playground. It is still worth looking around the fence yourself to see if there are small creatures under stones, spiders using the fence for their webs, and grass tufts housing other small creatures. If you find 'pockets' housing mini-beasts the children can be introduced to them.

Activity 3: Local parks and gardens
Visit a local park or ask a local resident who has a garden if you may visit. As in Activity 1, let the children look for, draw and name some of the plants and animals they

see there. Remind the children that parks and gardens (including the school garden) are worked on by people, and are not entirely 'natural habitats'. This means, for example, that compost dug into the school garden may attract creatures additional to those normally found there. Use this kind of information to show the children that humans have an effect on the environment. Take some photographs to form part of the children's record of their visit.

Area of study 33 | P of S 5a | LD 3

DETAILED HABITAT STUDY

Purpose
To show that physical differences and daily and seasonal changes are reflected in the kinds of plants and animals found in a location.

Materials needed
Fieldwork equipment such as clipboards and magnifiers, binoculars, collecting jars and bags; string and pegs for marking out observation areas.

Activity 1: The school perimeter fence
If your school has a lot of ground the children may not have explored along the perimeter fence or hedge. Using the perimeter fence or hedge as a location for study, ask each pair of children to take a marked out metre, or more if you wish. Get them to look for all they can find in that small area. They can collect specimens, but be sure to remind them of the care with which to work, and return the creatures to the hedge after they have been available for the children to see for a short while. Help the children to produce a 'picture map' of the hedge, with each pair of children contributing their section. On it they can attach some of the following:

- Drawings of creatures, with their measurements and other comments
- Names and descriptions of plants, bushes and trees
- Signs of birds and larger animals
- Any daily changes likely at the location (for example, for that part of the hedge next to the school gate, the constant use of the gateway at 8.50 a.m. and 3.30 p.m. might affect both plants and animals in different ways).

Area of study 34 | P of S 5a, b | LD 4

SURVIVAL AND SCARCE RESOURCES

C35

Purpose
To show that creatures only survive in habitats where their needs are adequately met, and that if resources become too scarce species have to move to another location, or become extinct.

Materials needed
A visiting garden expert, pictures and books about animals in their natural habitats; books about recently extinct species and information about wildlife in danger of extinction.

Activity 1: Plants
Ask a local gardening expert, or a colleague or parent who is a keen gardener to come and talk to the children about where cultivated plants are sited in order that they grow well. For example, smaller sun-loving plants are put at the front of borders rather than under the spreading branches of taller plants at the back which may exclude too much light. Plants with shallow root systems needing a lot of water may preclude the planting of others too close to them.

Activity 2: Animals
Choose some animals, locally occurring ones if possible, and talk about their needs in terms of the habitat required and why they live where they do.

Examples might include squirrels who live in parks where there are oak and hazel trees, birds of prey who often haunt fields of cereal crops, motorway verges where mice and other small mammals live and sea gulls, some of whom have sought a life inland where rubbish tips are a ready food supply for such scavengers.

Activity 3: Losers in the struggle to survive
If vital resources become scarce, animals move away or risk extinction. Find out about some of the creatures that have become extinct during the last two centuries. Ask the children to draw them and try to discover from the books why the creatures became extinct. Climatic changes, the loss of foodstuffs, humans' encroachment on habitats and hunting may all be possible reasons for extinction. Complete a 'recently extinct' dossier or create a home-made wallchart display.

Activity 4: Likely losers

Let the children choose a threatened species and find out all they can about its needs. It may be, for example, a bird, butterfly, whale or white rhino. The activity may be started with a display.

Ask them to devise a ten-point action plan to help prevent extinction. Invite someone from a local naturalists' trust or a local radio natural history team to come and give the children advice and help.

Copymaster 35 can be used to record their action plan.

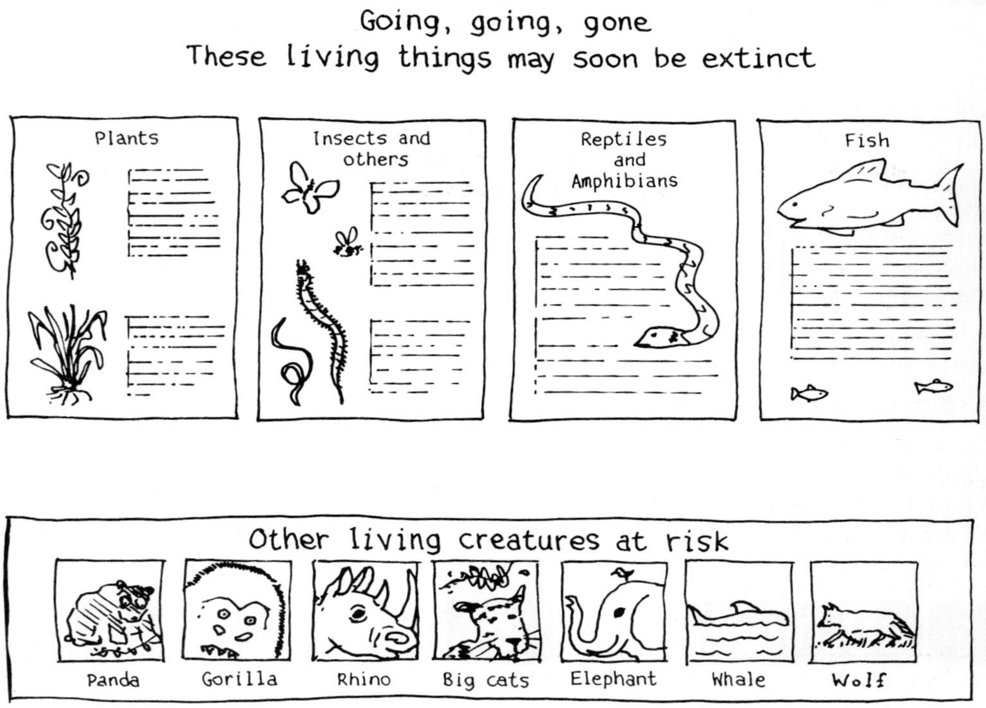

Area of study 35 | P of S 5a, b | LD 4

FOSSILS

C36, 37

Purpose

To show what fossils are and how they came about.

Materials needed

Books and charts about early life forms, museum exhibits including fossils and footprint casts, Plasticine® or clay; leaves, Vaseline®, hard plastic sheet, plaster of Paris; puppet making materials.

Activity 1: Fossils

Assemble a collection of fossils from a museum and/or borrowed from parents and children. Create a display (see the illustration on the next page).

Let the children examine and handle the fossils over a period of days. Then let them experiment with rubbings and chalks to produce accurate drawings.

Let the children use copymaster 36 to draw an outline of some fossils and do drawings of what they think the creatures looked like when alive.

Then label the fossils and the children can find out what they actually looked like. Discuss the kinds of creatures that might be preserved as fossils.

Activity 2: Coal

Look at a lump of coal and examine a time chart to find out how long ago the tree was alive. Some coal may contain leaf fossils.

Activity 3: Making plaster casts

Try making casts of foot and handprints and the prints of leaves to display alongside fossil print exhibits. There are casts of dinosaur prints to be seen in museums throughout the country. These would be a good source of comparison with those of members of the class! Make casts by placing a large lump of clay or Plasticine® in a shallow tray. Press the hand (or whatever is making the cast) into the clay. Fill the cast with plaster of Paris which has just been mixed. BE QUICK! It sets rapidly. Leave until hard, and peel off the clay.

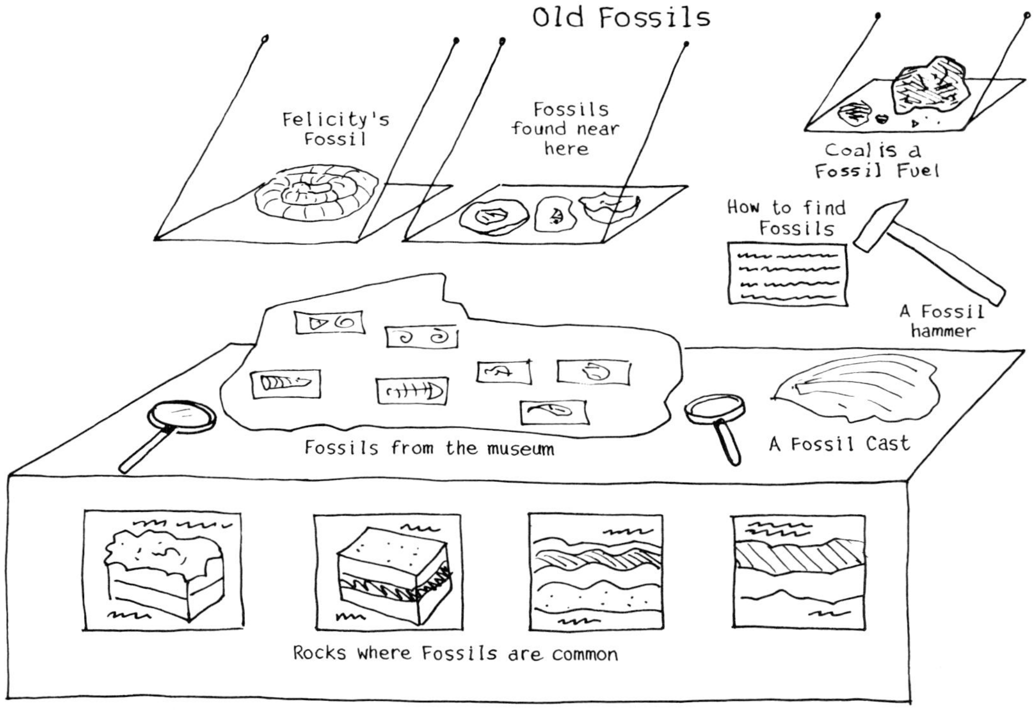

Activity 4: Making an imprint
Apply grease all over some leaves and place them on a plastic sheet. Build a 'boundary wall' of Plasticine® or clay a few centimetres high around the leaves. Pour in mixed plaster of Paris and leave until completely dry. Peel away the clay, turn over the plaster and lift off the leaves. There should be imprints of the leaves for the children to see. Some fossils were made by a layer of silt covering leaves or animals. The silt eventually hardened into sedimentary rock.

Activity 5: How fossils formed
Discuss with the children the ways in which fossils have been formed. These include those the children may already have talked about in Activities 1–4 above: the formation of a cast and carbonisation. Other methods include mineralisation of the bones and refrigeration (hence fossil mammoths).

Activity 6: Identifying the dinosaurs
If possible, before the children consult the secondary sources, let them do some detective work. Show them a cast of a dinosaur footprint or part of a bone and ask them to speculate on what the creature may have looked like. Get them to draw it and then show them what the experts think it looked like. Tell them what clues the experts used and what size the creature was, by comparing it with the school, a bus or something else of

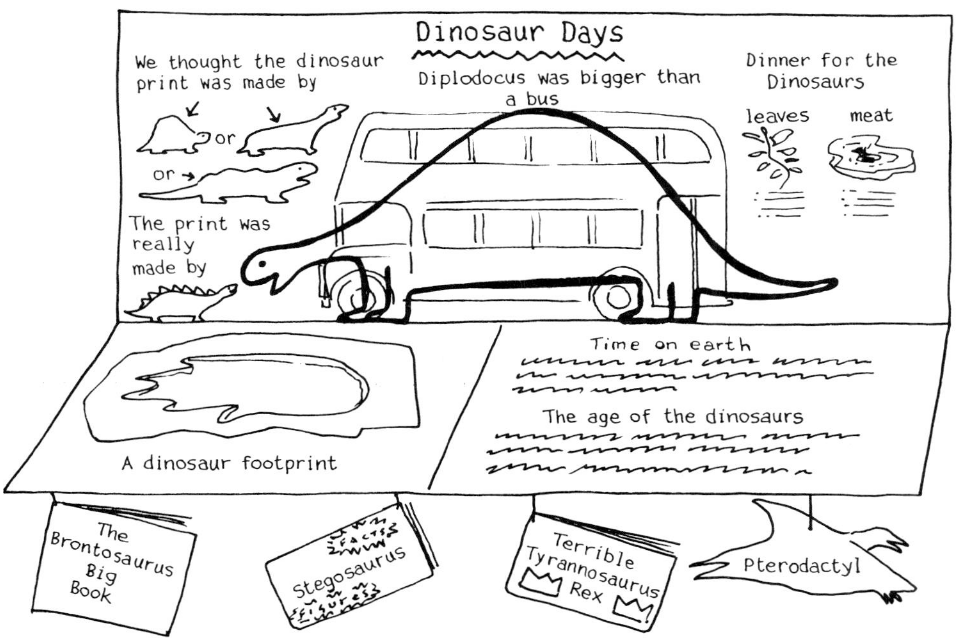

a suitable size. The children can then be placed in groups. Each group can choose a different dinosaur, research it and write about when it lived, its appearance, diet and how it moved. They can also try and trace where remains have been found and in which museums fossils are on show. The results of the enquiry can be entered in a group book which can be displayed and then consulted by all the children. It can be added to school resources.

Activity 7: The dinosaurs' demise
Ask the children to research possible reasons why there are no dinosaurs around today. They can be helped to make glove or stick puppets representing the Sun, swamp, named plants and, for example, a Stegosaurus, Pterodactyl and Tyrannosaurus Rex. They can then enact the possible set of circumstances which led to extinction. This is probably better scripted than left to improvisation and, if it turns out well, could be put on video for use with other groups.

Activity 8: Long-extinct but not a dinosaur
Invite a member of a museum's staff to come and talk to the children about long-extinct life forms such as the precursors of the horse. Alternatively, research this with the help of the children and get them to develop expertise on 'Creatures in the past'.

Copymaster 37 can be used for each child to record work about an extinct creature of their own choice, which may be, but need not necessarily be a dinosaur.

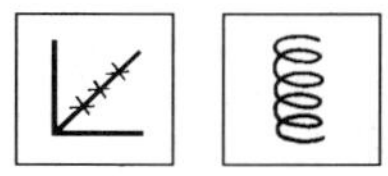

Area of study 36	P of S 5b	LD 4	COMPARING TWO HABITATS	C38

COMPARING TWO HABITATS

Purpose
To compare the flora and fauna of two different habitats, and to discuss how these living things are suited to their environment.

Materials needed
Fieldwork equipment, such as clipboards, magnifiers and binoculars.

Activity 1: Localities in the landscape
Depending on the location of the school, arrange trips to two locations where the children can look at plants and signs of animals in open country. This may, for example, be in a river valley, on a mountain, in woods, in dunes or near a beach. Let the children apply all their observation skills and record this information. This should offer the chance for them to make comparisons between things seen in these differing localities. For example:

- Do the trees have different shapes? Are they different kinds of tree?
- Where are we likely to find worms, leatherjackets or spiders?
- What sorts of birds can be seen in the open country location compared with those around school?

The children need to note down as many things as they can about each location. They may include some of the following:

- Type of soil
- Type of underlying rock

Animals and plants in two localities

- Landscape features (for example river basin, coastal dunes)
- Plants and trees
- Mini-beasts found
- Birds seen
- Signs of other animals
- Comments on daily changes occurring in each location
- Comments on what the seasonal changes are/are expected to be at the location.

The children can then set side by side their reports on the two locations and make comparisons.

Copymaster 38 allows the children to compare localities.

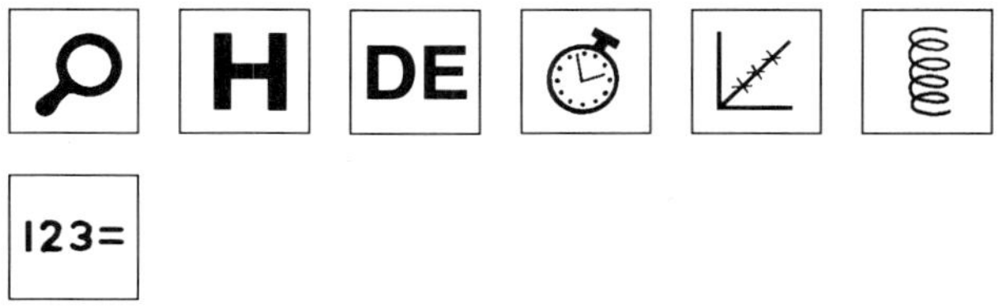

Activity 2: Comparing two countries
Using the reference books, choose two countries with widely differing terrain and climate. Ask the children to write a comparative study of the flora and fauna, relating the presence of these species to the physical conditions.

Programme of study: Life processes and living things

5. Living things in their environment

Pupils should be taught:

feeding relationships

c that food chains show feeding relationships in an ecosystem;

d that nearly all food chains start with a green plant.

Area of study 37 | P of S 5c, d | LD 4

FOOD CHAINS

Purpose
To explain the idea of a food chain.

Materials needed
Information packs about endangered species and reference books about food chains.

Activity: Food chains
Study food chains in the animal world, looking carefully at the diet, size, habitat and living habits of the creatures. The children should be aware of the delicate balance in nature between the species found in food chains.

Plants are the primary producers in food chains and all animals are directly or indirectly dependent on plants. Discuss the implications of this for the care of plant resources on our planet.

The children can also look at a wide variety of plants

and animals and establish whether they are part of a food chain or not. Not all animals are predators or prey.

Examples of food chains might include these:

Bird ⟶ caterpillar ⟶ cabbage
Snake ⟶ mouse ⟶ wheat

Finally the children can look at humans' place in relation to the natural world, and the human as predator for sport or gain. They can discuss and develop views on the endangered species and what action, if any, humans should take to prevent their extinction.

Programme of study: Life processes and living things

2. Living things and their environment

Pupils should be taught:

micro-organisms

e that micro-organisms exist, and that many may be beneficial, *e.g. in the breakdown of waste,* while others may be harmful, *e.g. in causing disease.*

Area of study 38 | P of S 5e | LD 3

COMPOST AND LEAF-MOULD

C39

Purpose
To look at compost and leaf-mould.

Materials needed
A see-through plastic bag containing some of the kinds of things we put on compost heaps, such a apple cores, potato peelings and tea-leaves; a bucket of 'mature' compost; fallen leaves, leaf-mould and fallen branches which have been on the ground some time.

NB Try to avoid putting these things in the dustbin when you have finished with them. In the interests of the environment they should be returned to the land, and the children should know this to.

Activity 1: Inspection of what is suitable for the compost
To avoid health risks, make a collection of things suitable for composting in a see-through bag and let the children look at the mixture through the bag. You can also cut up an apple and discard the pieces you do not wish to eat into the bag. The children can draw a set of things which will decay on the compost heap.

Copymaster 39 can be used to record what is suitable for the compost.

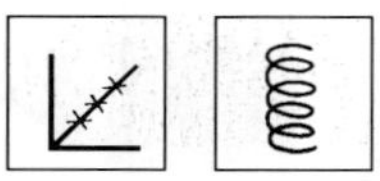

Activity 2: Inspection of mature compost
Wearing rubber gloves spread some garden compost on a sheet of newspaper. Without touching, the children can inspect the compost and see if they can identify what has gone into it. Tell them the age of the compost and what actually went into it.

Activity 3: Observation of the results of leaf decay
Show the children a collection of fallen leaves and some leaf-mould. Explain that leaf decay takes time. The children can draw a flow chart to show this process, as illustrated here.

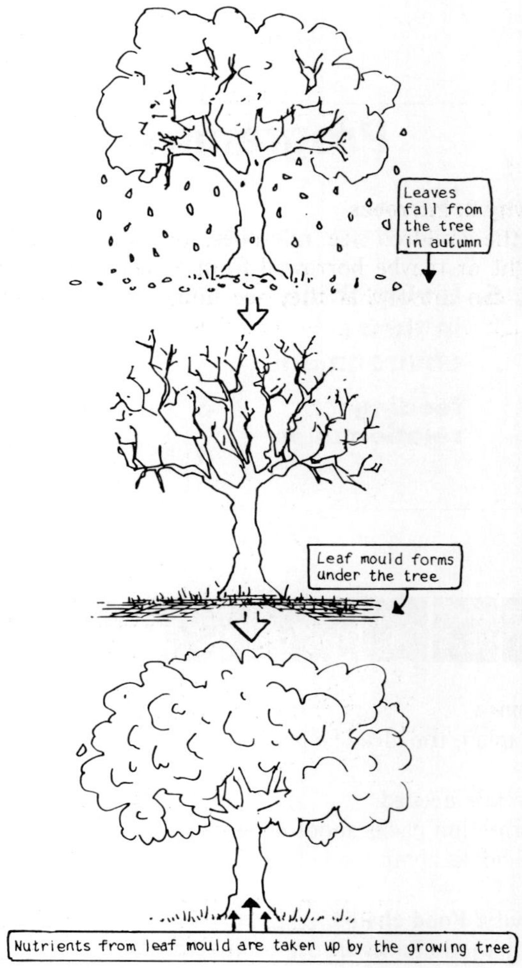

Activity 4: Decay in the woods
Take a walk in the woods if you can, and observe what is happening to the fallen leaves and branches. If there are no woods near school collect some partially decayed wood, and display it in class for the children to see and talk about. Then tell the children that you are going to return the wood to the woods from which it came, and do just that.

Area of study 39 | P of S 5e | LD 5

DECAY AND MICROBES

Purpose
To identify what happens when things decay.

Materials needed
Compost, flowerpots, sunflower or cress seeds; microscope slides of microbes.

Activity 1: An investigation of compost heaps
Consult the health and safety regulations before children dig in! Discuss the compost heaps they may have seen or have in their own garden. What do they think happens? Get them to ask someone who has a compost heap what he/she thinks happens. Try to obtain some mature, well-rotted compost and grow some sunflower seeds or cress in it alongside pots containing seeds in ordinary soil. The vigorous growth they see in the seeds growing in compost will help them to understand the circular process of decay and regeneration and the necessity, for example, of leaving rotten branches and dead leaves in the woods, so that the woods themselves survive. Tell the children about the work of the small creatures in the compost, and the sort of conditions they need to assist decomposition.

Activity 2: Microbes
Let the children see microbes, on slides you have bought or maybe borrowed from a secondary school. They can draw what they see under the microscope. Though it is easy to grow microbes in the classroom we do not recommend it as you should be certain that there is no health risk whatsoever before you do so, and that may be difficult to guarantee. You can tell the children about the growth of microbes in the laboratory. Tell them that some microbes are beneficial and some harmful.

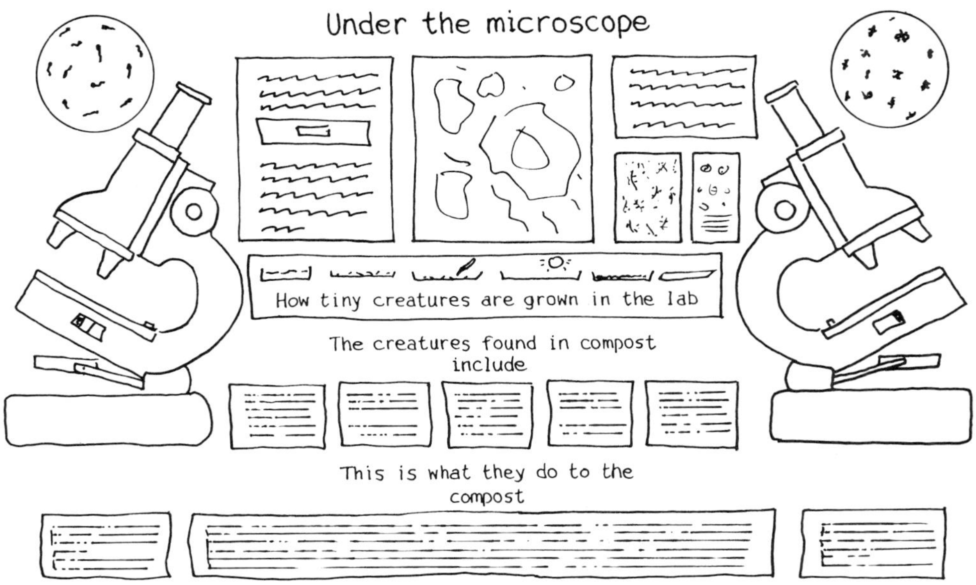

Materials and their properties

How the Areas of study in this book relate to the section of the Programme of study and Attainment target level descriptions. Programme of study		Areas of study and 'best fit' with Level descriptions			
		Level description 2	**Level description 3**	**Level description 4**	**Level description 5**
1. Grouping and classifying materials	Pupils should be taught: **a** to compare everyday materials, *e.g. wood, rock, iron, aluminium, paper, polythene,* on the basis of their properties, including hardness, strength, flexibility and magnetic behaviour, and to relate these properties to everyday uses of the materials;	Area of study: 1	Areas of study: 2, 3		
	b that some materials are better thermal insulators than others;		Area of study: 4		
	c that some materials are better electrical conductors than others;		Area of study: 5		
	d to describe and group rocks and soils on the basis of characteristics, including appearance, texture and permeability;			Area of study: 6	
	e to recognise differences between solids, liquids and gases, in terms of ease of flow and maintenance of shape and volume.			Area of study: 7	
2. Changing materials	**a** that mixing materials, *e.g. adding salt to water,* can cause them to change;	Area of study: 8			
	b that heating or cooling materials, *e.g. water, clay, dough,* can cause them to change, and that temperature is a measure of how hot or cold they are;	Area of study: 9	Area of study: 10		
	c that some changes can be reversed and some cannot;	Area of study: 9	Areas of study: 11, 12		
	d that dissolving, melting, boiling, condensing, freezing and evaporating are changes that can be reversed;		Area of study: 11		

Materials and their properties

How the Areas of study in this book relate to the section of the Programme of study and Attainment target level descriptions.			Areas of study and 'best fit' with Level descriptions			
Programme of study						
		Pupils should be taught:	**Level description 2**	**Level description 3**	**Level description 4**	**Level description 5**
	e	about the water cycle and the part played by evaporation and condensation;			Area of study: 13	
	f	that the changes that occur when most materials, *e.g. wood, wax, natural gas,* are burned are not reversible.			Area of study: 14	
3. Separating mixtures of materials	**a**	that solid particles of different sizes, *e.g. those in soils,* can be separated by sieving;	Area of study: 15			
	b	that some solids, *e.g. salt, sugar,* dissolve in water to give solutions but some, *e.g. sand, chalk,* do not;			Area of study: 16	
	c	that insoluble solids can be separated from liquids by filtering;			Area of study: 16	Area of study: 17
	d	that solids that have dissolved can be recovered by evaporating the liquid from the solution;				Area of study: 17
	e	that there is a limit to the mass of solid that can dissolve in a given amount of water, and that this limit is different for different solids.				Area of study: 18

Level descriptions: Materials and their properties

Level 2

Pupils identify a range of common materials and know about some of their properties. They describe similarities and differences between materials. They sort materials into groups and describe in everyday terms, such as shininess, hardness or smoothness, the basis for their groupings. They describe ways in which some materials are changed by heating or cooling or by processes such as bending or stretching.

Level 3

Pupils use their knowledge and understanding of materials when they describe a variety of ways of sorting them into groups according to their properties. They explain why some materials are particularly suitable for specific purposes, such as a metal for making electrical cables. They recognise that some changes, such as the freezing of water, can be reversed and some, such as the baking of clay, cannot, and they classify changes in this way.

Level 4

Pupils demonstrate knowledge and understanding of aspects of Materials and their properties drawn from the Key Stage 2 or Key Stage 3 Programme of Study. They describe differences between the properties of different materials and explain how these differences are used to classify substances as solids, liquids and gases. They describe some methods, such as filtration, that are used to separate simple mixtures. They use scientific terms, such as evaporation or condensation, to describe changes. They use knowledge about some reversible and irreversible changes to make simple predictions about whether other changes are reversible or not.

Level 5

Pupils demonstrate an increasing knowledge and understanding of aspects of Materials and their properties drawn from the Key Stage 2 or Key Stage 3 Programme of Study. They describe some metallic properties, such as good electrical conductivity, and use these properties to distinguish metals from other solids. They identify a range of contexts in which changes, such as evaporation or condensation, take place. They use knowledge about how a specific mixture, such as salt and water, or sand and water, can be separated to suggest ways in which other similar mixtures might be separated.

Programme of study: Materials and their properties

Work on solids, liquids and gases should be related to pupils' observations of changes that take place when materials are heated and cooled, and to ways in which mixtures can be separated.

1. Grouping and classifying materials

Pupils should be taught:

a to compare everyday materials, *e.g. wood, rock, iron, aluminium, paper, polythene,* on the basis of their properties, including hardness, strength, flexibility and magnetic behaviour, and to relate these properties to everyday uses of the materials;

b that some materials are better thermal insulators than others;

- **c** that some materials are better electrical conductors than others;
- **d** to describe and group rocks and soils on the basis of characteristics, including appearance, texture and permeability;
- **e** to recognise differences between solids, liquids and gases; in terms of ease of flow and maintenance of shape and volume.

Area of study 1 | P of S 1a | LD 2

CHARACTERISTICS OF MATERIALS

C40, 41

Purpose
To identify some of the characteristics of materials.

Materials needed
A collection of naturally occurring and manufactured materials, for example, rocks and pebbles, wood, straw, rubber, metal strips, clay, pottery, fabrics, glass, plastic; magnets.

Activity 1: Comparison of materials
Assemble and lay out a collection of at least five kinds of material. Let the children handle the materials and compare them according to criteria they have decided on themselves. Discuss how they have decided to sort them. Arrange the sorted items in a display. The following day ask the children to try sorting again, but differently. Repeat this process until the children have established many kinds of 'sort'.

The children can draw some examples of materials with various properties on copymaster 40.

Activity 2: The concept of transparency
Let the children look at a variety of glass and plastic samples. If necessary, tape the edges to prevent the children cutting themselves. You will need plain glass, patterned glass, frosted glass, coloured glass and opaque glass; see-through plastic, coloured plastic and opaque plastic. Packaging such as a jam jar, green and brown bottles and the plastic found in biscuit or chocolate boxes is of use, but you will also need to acquire some offcuts from a glazier. If they do not already know, explain the concept of transparency to them and get them to rank the samples in order of transparency. Ask them why we need some things to be transparent. Get them to name things in their home which are transparent.

Activity 3: Rank samples according to a characteristic
Choose a broad range of materials and ask the children to rank them in terms of hardness, flexibility (will they bend or stretch and spring back) and transparency in turn. The children can tabulate their results by drawing each item where it fits in the ranking.

Copymaster 41 can be used to record this work.

Activity 4: Magnetic attraction
Ask the children to use a magnet on the sample materials to find out which are attracted by it. These should be placed in a set. Explain that they all contain the mineral iron.

Area of study 2 | P of S 1a | LD 3 | C42

LINKING PROPERTIES AND USES

Purpose
To link the properties of some materials to their uses.

Materials needed
Some examples of what might be included are: rocks and pebbles; wood, wooden objects such as a bowl and a piece of carved wood, a wooden spoon and a ruler; paper of various kinds; straw and willow, e.g. used in a basket; rubber sheeting and a ball, eraser, rubber bands and a plimsoll; metals including rock containing ore, a tin can, a steel rule, watch parts and parts of a machine such as a bike or car; clay, pottery and china; clothes and linens made of natural fibres such as wool and cotton, and manufactured fibres, e.g. nylon, including dishcloths and tights; glass pieces of various colours ranging from transparent to opaque; plastic containers and extruded packaging, plastic bottles and sheeting.

Activity: Comparing characteristics and uses
The characteristics of materials determine their uses. For the children to begin to understand this, they need to 'match' a raw material to a 'use'. Give them objects such as a piece of rubber sheet and a ball, a log and a stool, a rock containing metal (such as iron ore) and a large bolt, and get them to do the matching. Display the resulting 'matches', and reasons for them.

Copymaster 42 can be used for the children to make their own record of the match between raw materials and uses.

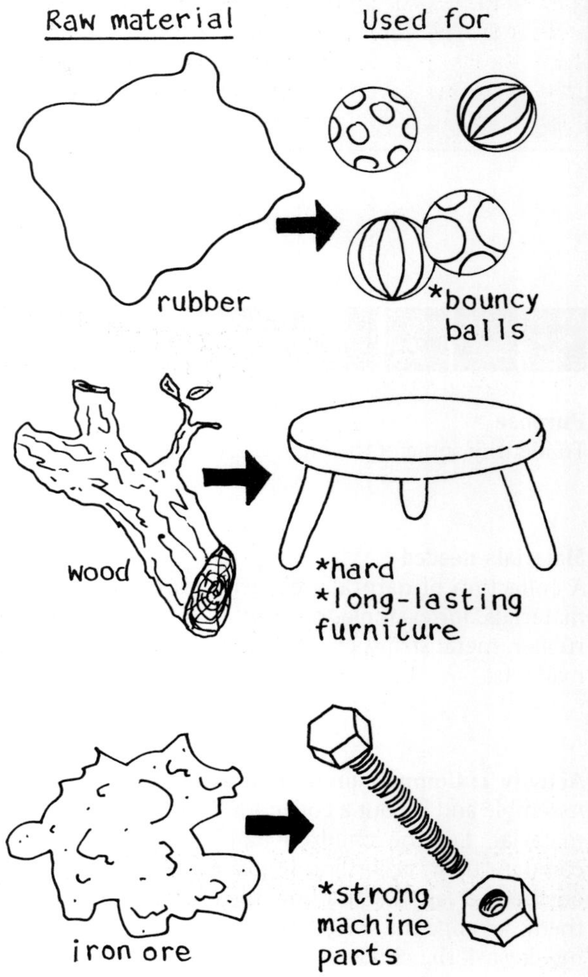

Area of study 3 | P of S 1a | LD 3 | C43, 44

NATURAL AND MANUFACTURED MATERIALS

Purpose
To show that some materials are found naturally while others have to be made.

Materials needed
Assemble a collection of materials similar to those used in the previous Area of study.

Activity 1: What is natural and what is manufactured?
Give the children a range of natural and manufactured materials, trying not to put in 'finished' products such as crockery or clothes (see Activity 2). Let the children sort the materials into two sets: natural and manufactured. They can leave to one side the things they are not sure about. Discuss their groupings with them and help them with uncertainties.

They can record their groupings on copymaster 43.

Activity 2: Finished products using natural and other materials
Give the children a range of raw materials, samples of these materials prepared for manufacture and samples of finished products. The intention is that children should understand that humans change natural and manufactured materials to produce the things we use. For example, you can include in the collection a fleece, a ball of wool and a jumper; a cotton boll, a reel of cotton thread and a skirt or tea-towel; a piece of iron ore, a metal ingot and a nut and bolt; a log, a plank and

a stool; the content of a kit for making plastic paper weights (make sure that the children do not open and handle these, as they contain harmful chemicals), plastic sheeting or shredded packaging and a comb or toothbrush; clay and a flowerpot. Let the children put these things in order from raw materials to finished product. You may then like to show them mixed products such as costume jewellery and shoes. Display the children's work. Discuss why the raw materials are so used and the reasons why, for example, we do not wear wooden vests or make wool into nuts and bolts!

The children can use copymaster 44 to record the flow from raw materials to finished products.

123=

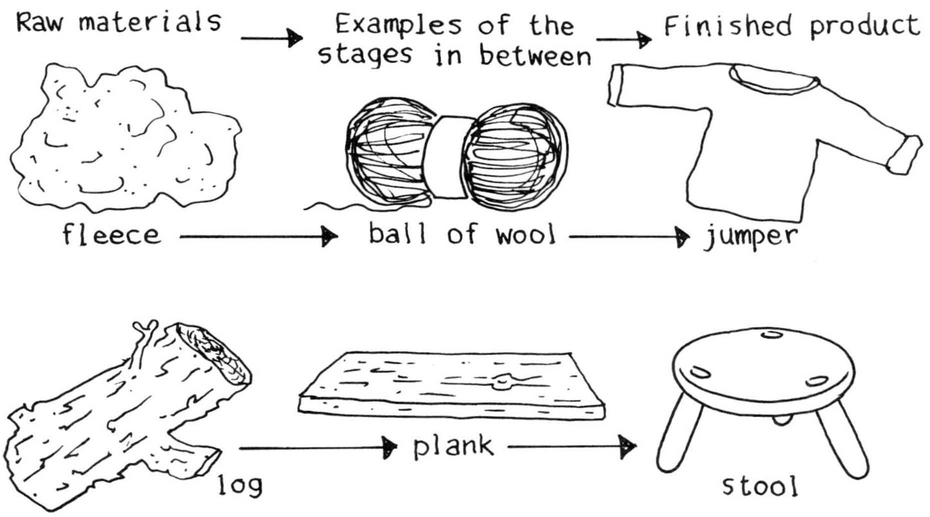

Area of study 4 | P of S 1b | LD 3

THERMAL INSULATION

C45, 46

Purpose
To show that some materials offer thermal insulation.

Materials needed
Plastic beakers, scraps of different types of material.

Activity 1: Keeping warm
Tell the children that we help our bodies to stay warm by insulating them with clothes.

With the children, look at their outdoor clothes on a cool day. Contrast what we need to wear outdoors on a winter's day compared with a summer's day to keep our bodies at the right temperature.

Let each child draw him/herself wearing winter and summer clothes on copymaster 45.

Activity 2: Heat insulation
Discuss the idea that clothing keeps us warm, as in Activity 1, and cool, as when doing PE. Then set up an experiment to find out the kinds of materials which will keep in heat energy and those which allow heat energy loss. Wrap similar plastic beakers or bottles containing hot water in various kinds of material, including wool, cotton, plastic, paper and nylon. Feel each container periodically to check which one seems to be cooling down quickest.

The children can record this experiment on copymaster 46.

H DE 123=

Set up a display of clothes we wear and the results of Activity 2.

Area of study 5 | P of S 1c | LD 3

GOOD AND BAD CONDUCTORS

C47

Purpose
To show that some materials are good conductors of electricity and others are not.

Materials needed
Circuit-making materials, including wire, wire cutters, lamp in holder, compatible battery, press-on terminals, crocodile clips and a variety of materials to try in the circuit, such as a pencil, a necklace, a cereal packet or other cardboard box, a potato, glass, plastic, pottery, keys, a shoe (in fact any inanimate object to which crocodile clips can be attached).

Activity 1: Good/bad conductors
Make up a circuit including the battery and the lamp and attach crocodile clips to the free ends of the wire, as shown.

Let the children have a try at completing the circuit by connecting a variety of materials in turn. Those that are good conductors will permit a current to pass which will be sufficient to light the lamp. Poor conductors may light the lamp very dimly, and many materials will appear to be bad conductors.

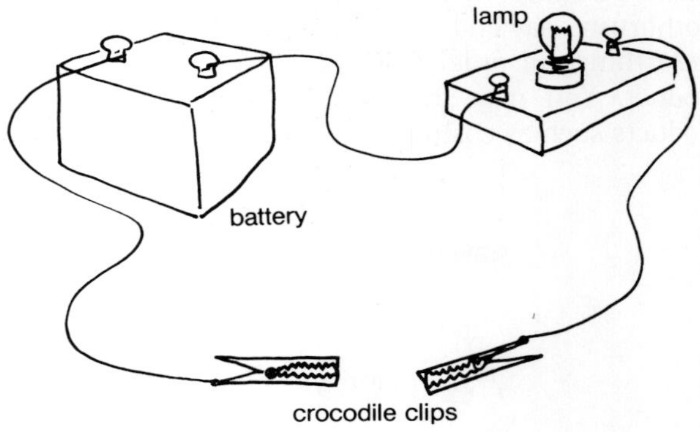

The children can record this investigation on copymaster 47.

Area of study 6 | P of S 1d | LD 4

ROCKS AND SOILS

C48, 49

Purpose
To understand the factors producing different sediments and soils.

Materials needed
A collection of rock and soil samples of varying hue, texture, hardness and colour; magnifiers and 'dibbers'; slides, film or video showing the effects of weathering.

Activity 1: A range of rocks and soils
To open the children's discussion of this subject in detail, arrange a display of a wide variety of rocks and soil samples. Try to include some that are unfamiliar to the children. Supply magnifiers and 'dibbers' and let the children examine the samples and speculate on the kind of terrain the rocks may come from, and the likely resulting kinds of soils. An example of this type of display is shown on the next page.

Activity 2: Effects of water, wind and ice
Discuss the effects of water, wind and ice on the landscape, including the following effects:

- Erosion and transport by seas and rivers
- Wind effects in carrying light material to new locations
- Glacial effects in the past on our landscape.

View slides or film or video showing the effects of weathering.

Activity 3: Weathering and soils
Let children examine rock and 'matching' soil specimens. Let them feel it, look at it under the magnifier, pour water into the rock and into the matching soil sample to test how porous it is (does water run through or is it absorbed?). Weigh samples of several soils (the same volume of each, perhaps that filling a small flowerpot) and compare the soils to see whether they are dense and compact or light and friable. Discuss which might be the more fertile of soils. Grow a bean, a couple of nasturtium seeds, mustard and cress or sunflowers in each soil sample and note how long germination takes in each. Which turn out to be the more fertile soils? Do they have common properties described by the children in their earlier investigations?

You can use copymaster 48 to record findings (use a new sheet for each different seed grown).

Activity 4: Looking at weathering
Take the children on a trip to see parts of the local landscape where weathering, erosion and transport are occurring.

Copymaster 49 gives the children the opportunity to compile a report about the effects of water, wind and ice on the landscape.

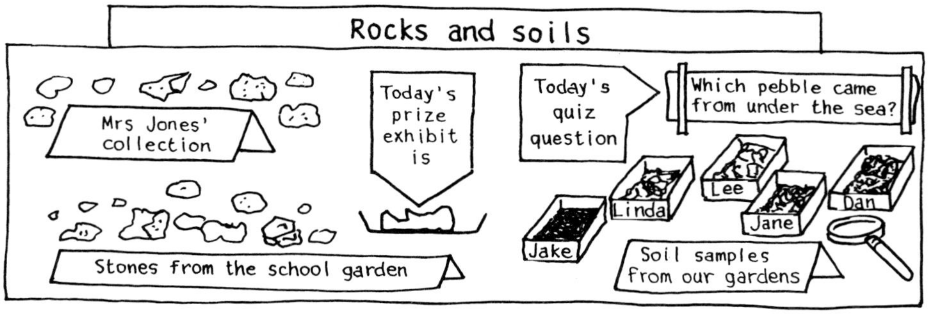

Area of study 7 | P of S 1a, e | LD 4

SOLIDS, LIQUIDS AND GASES

C50–52

Purpose
To investigate some of the properties of solids, liquids and gases.

Materials needed
A collection of raw materials including: cotton thread, nylon fishing line, a ball of wool, elastic, wire in a variety of gauges ranging from fuse to garden wire, a hacksaw blade, a short length of rope of the type that may be used to support a swing, a short length of garden hose, a variety of rocks, pieces of plastic, coins, paper art straws, plastic straws and sets of gramme masses; small clamps, books with pictures about architectural styles in history, bridges and building.

A variety of 'hard' materials in pieces suitable for putting on classroom balances, including at least two samples of similar size and shape, preferably of different metals; balances and masses; a plastic vivarium filled with water with graduations on the side, and/or plastic measuring jugs of water; a bottle of milk, an empty milk bottle, bottles or cans of fizzy drinks and similar empty bottles or cans, a bottle of washing-up liquid and a similar empty bottle, an accurate and sensitive balance or scales.

Activity 1: Strength and shape
If possible take the children to look at a variety of buildings, noting in particular the materials used and the shapes of archways, doorways and shapes used in the construction of, for example, roofs in churches, factories, barns, railway stations. The children can also consult secondary sources such as books, photographs and film to identify the kinds of material and shape used in construction. Their research should show a pattern of the common use of triangles and curves. They can investigate further why such shapes are 'strong' ones. They can also record which materials are in common use in building construction, and why. It is possible to tie in this work with their activities in Design and Technology.

Copymaster 50 gives children the chance to identify strong shapes and draw them.

Activity 2: Strength and loads
Stronger materials do support heavier loads, and the children will already be able to predict that plastic is stronger than paper and that metals are stronger still. A test to confirm the paper-plastic comparison can be done by clamping a drinking straw made from each of these two materials in turn between two desks and suspending masses from them. Add the masses to a plastic or fabric bag, and test until the paper straw breaks or buckles permanently. If you can add one more mass to the plastic straw than could be supported by the paper straw, this will indicate that the plastic straw is stronger. The children can list some examples of the use of strong materials to carry loads, e.g. roads, bridges, girders, HGVs. Tell them that it is in fact a combination of strength and shape which enables structures to carry loads.

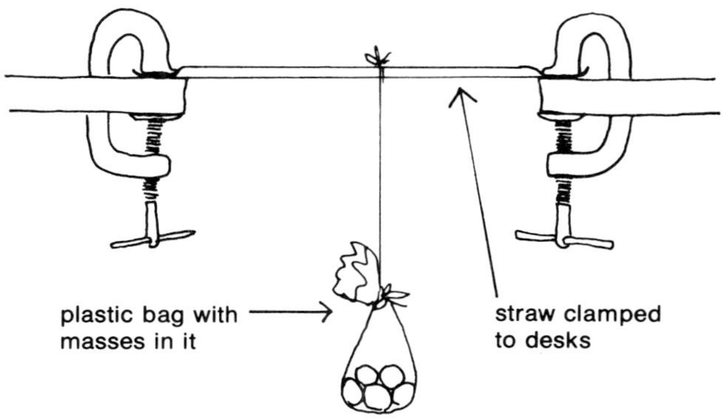

Activity 3: Hardness of different materials
Lay out a range of materials which feel 'hard', such as chalk, flint, granite, limestone, 'local' rock, slate, brick,

concrete, plastic, glass, pottery, coins, metal bars. Let the children handle and inspect the samples, and then devise a strategy for systematically testing which material will make a scratch on all the others. The children should be able to find the hardest material, and rank all the others.

Their results can be tabulated on copymaster 51.

Activity 4: Playground hardness
Discuss with the children the surfaces available for them to play on at school and the surfaces they have seen in children's play areas. Discuss what it must be like to fall over on each of these surfaces, and therefore which is judged to be the hardest. The discussion may include the following list of surfaces: grass, bare earth, tarmac, concrete, bark and the special 'soft' surface which has been introduced under the equipment in some playgrounds. This work can link to an investigation of hardness and road surfacing.

Activity 5: Flexibility of different materials
A variety of materials need to be tested to see which return to their original shape when bent or stretched. The children can suspend a length of each of the following materials in turn from a clamp, the edge of the desk, or a cup hook in the wall: cotton, nylon fishing line, elastic and springs (which they can make from different kinds of wire). In each case they need to measure the length of the suspended material and mark where the end of the material comes. Masses are then put on a hanger suspended from the end in an attempt to achieve some stretch. Then the masses can be taken off and the children can note whether the material returns to its original length. The children can then list some everyday uses of elastic materials, e.g. fishing line, watch springs, washing line, curtain wire, socks.

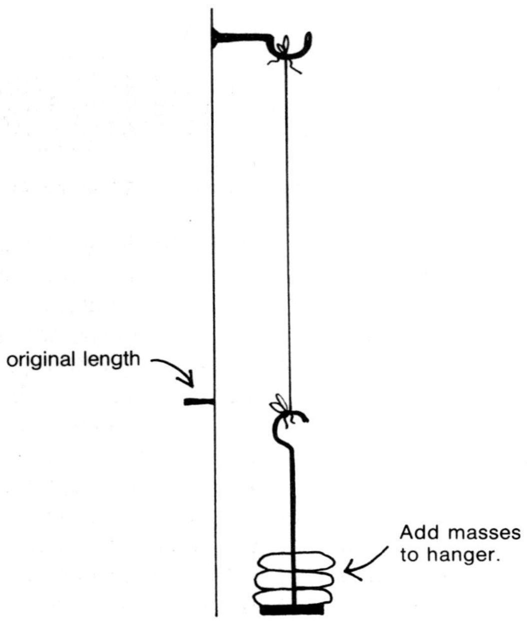

Activity 6: New inventions
Ask the children to invent some things and to decide themselves what materials the things should be made from. They must give their reasons for the choice of material. Examples might include a flask to keep drinks hot, a roller boot, a pop-up birthday card, a carrying case for cassettes, running shoes, swimwear, a moveable toy suitable for a two-year-old.

The children can record their inventions on copymaster 52.

Activity 7: Solids have weight and volume
The children can weigh some pieces of sample material and then, having read off the water level in a tank or jug, they can lower the sample into it and work out from the new water level the amount of water that has been displaced. Wood, polystyrene and other materials which float will have to be held beneath the surface of the water with a pencil.

Activity 8: Similar size means similar volume
Similar-sized pieces, e.g. cubes or bars, of different materials will displace the same amount of water. If they are then weighed they will not weigh the same. The children can speculate on why this is so, and should be helped to understand that the difference is due to differences in density between materials.

Activity 9: Liquids have weight and volume
Weigh full and empty milk bottles, drinks cans and washing-up liquid bottles. The difference between the measurements is the weight of the liquid. Immerse the full and empty vessels in a tank of water and there will be more water displaced by the full ones. The difference in water levels will be due mostly to the liquid in the full bottle or can. Point out that this is not accurate, for even the empty containers have walls of plastic or glass, for example, which may be quite thick; even the walls of vessels have volume. Ask the children how they can determine the volume of the bottle or can. They should be able to tell from the contents printed on the container the volume of liquid inside, and work out the volume of the container itself from their figures.

Activity 10: Weighing carbon dioxide
The children can see from containers of fizzy drink that the drinks contain the gas carbon dioxide to make them fizzy. If they weigh the full containers and then take the cap or ring pull off and leave the drink to go flat they can weigh it again. The difference in 'weight' is the 'weight' of gas put into the drink.

Programme of study: Materials and their properties

2. Changing materials

Pupils should be taught:

a that mixing materials, *e.g. adding salt to water,* can cause them to change;

b that heating or cooling materials, *e.g. water, clay, dough,* can cause them to change, and that temperature is a measure of how hot or cold they are;

c that some changes can be reversed and some cannot;

d that dissolving, melting, boiling, condensing, freezing and evaporating are changes that can be reversed;

e about the water cycle and the part played by evaporation and condensation;

f that the changes that occur when most materials, *e.g. wood, wax, natural gas,* are burned are not reversible.

Area of study 8 | P of S 2a | LD 2

MIXING MATERIALS

Purpose
To find out what happens when materials are mixed together.

Materials needed
Biscuit ingredients as follows: 175 g plain flour, 50 g sugar, 100 g butter, 2 drops vanilla essence; mixing bowl, baking tray and access to oven, beaker, salt, water, sugar, milk, milk-shake granules.

Activity 1: Mixing biscuit dough
Encourage the children to look at and feel what happens when the butter is rubbed into the flour. How does the appearance and consistency of the ingredients change when they are mixed?

The sugar and vanilla can be stirred into the rubbed-in (breadcrumb-like) mixture. Kneading produces a dough. This can be rolled out, cut into rounds and baked at 170°C for 20 minutes.

Activity 2: Mixing solutions
What happens when the children add salt to water, sugar to water and milk-shake granules to cold milk? They should describe the changes.

Area of study 9 | P of S 2b,c,d | LD 2

EFFECTS OF HEATING AND COOLING

C53

Purpose
To show that materials sometimes change when warmed or cooled, and that the change can be permanent.

Materials needed
Fimo® or home-made play dough (made with two cups of flour to one of salt, with water and a little oil to mix, and some cream of tartar to stop it being sticky), ice-cubes and a freezer or freezer compartment of the fridge to re-freeze them, a candle in a holder and matches, a large bar of chocolate, plain biscuits, a saucepan and a wooden spoon, baking parchment, a table jelly, boiling water, a measuring jug and a bowl or individual containers (to set the jelly in).

Activity 1: What happens to model dough when we heat it?
Make some models from Fimo® or play dough. Fimo® is expensive but the colours are vivid and it holds its shape perfectly. Play dough is cheap but very soft and elastic, and it may prove difficult to make detailed impressions on it. The children could make models depicting some aspect of their work in other subjects. When the models are finished they need to be baked in an oven. Fimo® carries instructions. Play dough needs slow baking. The models can be painted and varnished. The children will observe that the dough which was soft and malleable retains neither of these characteristics after baking and in fact it becomes quite hard and brittle. This change is permanent. Display some raw dough and the finished models.

Activity 2: The effects of heat and cold on water
Carefully heat some water in a pan or kettle without an automatic switch. As the water approaches boiling point discuss what happens when it boils. When it has been boiling for some time the children will be able to observe the steam and see that the level of the water in the pan has gone down (wait until it cools to show them this). Some of the water has 'gone'. Tell them that the steam is water vapour. As the water vapour cools it will turn back into water on cool surfaces such as the windows.

Now pour some water into an ice-tray and put it into the freezer or freezer compartment of the fridge to cool. When ice starts to form, get it out and show the children. Then return it to the freezer until cubes form. Take the ice-tray out. Put the ice-cubes into a bowl and observe what happens when they are left at room temperature. Discuss with the children the idea that liquid water becomes solid if it is made very cold, and turns back to liquid when warmed again.

Activity 3: The effect of heat on candle wax
Taking care that the children are at a safe distance, light a household candle. As the wax melts the children can see that it becomes liquid. You can let liquid drops drip on to a sheet of paper. When they are cool the children can see that as the hot wax cools it turns solid again.

Activity 4: The effect of heat on chocolate
Though the children will already be familiar with this, it is fun to do, and may therefore establish the solid-liquid-solid chain concept more readily than other experiments. Break the chocolate into a bowl and stand the bowl in a pan of hot water. Heat the pan if necessary to melt the chocolate. In order that everyone may have a taste, you may find it easiest to dip one end of some plain biscuits in the chocolate and lay them on baking parchment to cool. Alternatively, stir some cornflakes or rice krispies into the chocolate, and when bound together spoon out little mounds onto the baking parchment then leave them to set. Before they eat the evidence, make sure that the children have noted that solid chocolate melts to a liquid when heated and returns to solid when cooled.

Activity 5: The effect of heat on jelly
Show the children an unmade table jelly, or one that has been made up and set in a bowl. Make up the jelly according to the instructions, or tip the made up jelly into a pan and heat it until it melts. Then put the jelly into individual containers and leave to set. (One table jelly will make about eight small helpings). The children can take the jelly home for tea. They will also have noted that solid jelly, when warmed, becomes liquid and when cooled, becomes solid again.

To record their work in Activities 2 to 5 they can compile a table of results on copymaster 53.

H

Area of study 10 | P of S 2b | LD 3

TEMPERATURE

C54, 55

Purpose
To establish that temperature is a measure of hot or cold.

Materials needed
Hot and cold water, two beakers and a bowl; temperature indicator strips, Celsius thermometer with easily visible column, a maximum and minimum thermometer, a clinical thermometer; a variety of cups and beakers and a large jug containing a hot drink.

Activity 1: Human judgement and temperature
Put hot water into one beaker, cold into the other and warm water into the bowl. Let the children, each in turn, put one hand into the hot water, the other into the cold and then both into the warm water. They should find that the warm water feels cold on the hand that has been in hot, and hot on the hand that has been in cold. Tell the children that this shows that we are not always good at judging heat and cold. We need instruments to help us.

Activity 2: Temperature indicators
Show the children a temperature indicator strip, suitable for use in finding out whether a small child is running a temperature, meaning that he/she is unwell. Show the children what it does and try it out.

Activity 3: Thermometers
Let the children see and handle a Celsius thermometer. Ask them what it is for. Tell them that when the liquid in the bulb gets warmer, the liquid expands. The only space it can move to is the stem of the thermometer, so up it goes. Then let them see a maximum and minimum thermometer. Discuss where these may be useful, including greenhouses and weather stations. Finally, show them a clinical thermometer, noting that the scale is different and that there is a kink in the stem. The children can draw and label the thermometers, and explain why the scales and/or ranges of temperature vary.

Activity 4: Measuring air temperature
Show the children how to read a thermometer, with the indicating level at eye level. Let them investigate temperature change at school, controlling some of the variables. For example, they may use a fixed site, or a certain height above ground; they may record only indoors or only outside. It may be a good idea to place a number of thermometers around the school, and at fixed times let the children go off and read them.

The children can write down their efforts on copymaster 54.

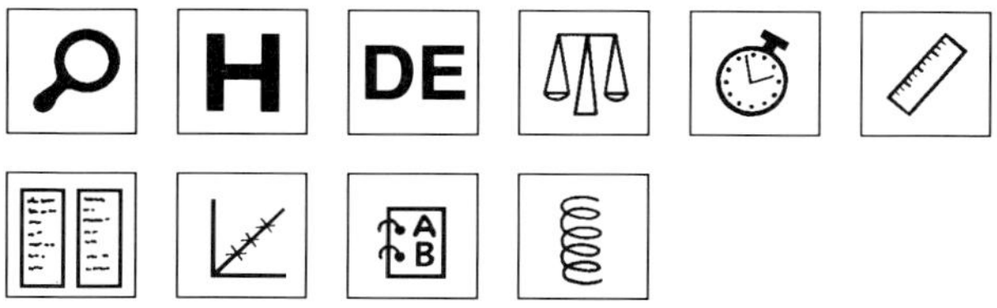

Activity 5: Measuring the temperature of liquids
Let the children try to discover what shape of cup keeps a drink hot the longest by pouring a hot drink into a number of cups, mugs and beakers. The temperature of the drink must then be taken at regular intervals. You may also discuss the relevance of the material the cups and mugs are made of.

Results from this experiment can be recorded on copymaster 55.

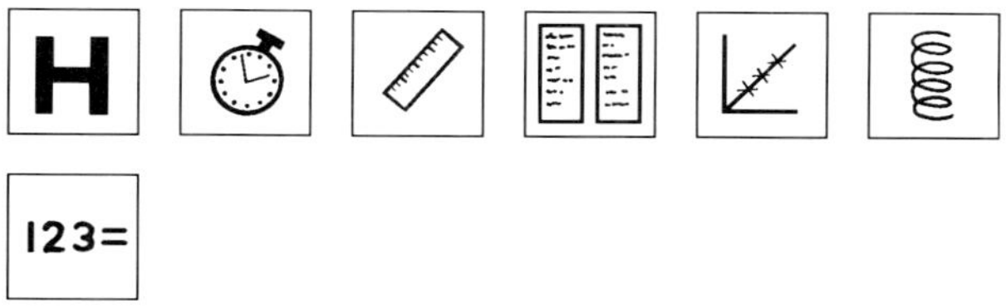

Activity 6: Heating raises temperature and cooling lowers it
The children know this! But to prove it, they can take the temperature of some water or milk and then, under supervision, heat the liquid in a pan. The temperature of the liquid can be read every couple of minutes. They can then reverse the experiment, going below room temperature by putting the liquid in the fridge.

Activity 7: Heat can cause expansion, cooling contraction
Discuss examples of this in the children's experience: hot feet may mean shoes feel tight, cakes come out of the tin more easily if left to cool slightly first. Then demonstrate these phenomena by making popcorn and looking at, for example, custard which has been allowed to go cold: the level of the hot custard can be seen on the side of the jug, above the present 'cold level'. (Note that water turning to ice is a notable exception to the rule.) If the school has a bar breaker now is the time to use it.

Activity 8: Heat-sensitive equipment
Discuss the fact that the fire service and other emergency services sometimes need to use heat sensitive 'cameras' to detect whether anyone is trapped in collapsed buildings. The camera is sensitive to the heat energy given out by the live human being.

Area of study 11	P of S 2c, d	LD 3	**REVERSIBLE CHANGE**	C56

Purpose
To explain the common chain solid–liquid–gas which occurs when some materials are subjected to heat or cold.

Materials needed
Tap water, ice-cube tray, freezer, Celsius thermometers, saucers, bowls and jugs, a kettle full of water, a candle in a suitable holder and matches.

Activity 1: Effects of heat and cold on water
The children can measure the temperature of tap water. They can pour some of this water into an ice-tray and set it to freeze in a freezer or fridge cold compartment. As ice starts to form they can take the tray out and measure the temperature again. Return the tray to the freezer. When ice-cubes have formed take the tray out and empty the ice into a bowl. The children can observe the ice melting as it returns to room temperature. They can measure the temperature periodically during the melting process. That same water, heated in the kettle, will boil, turn to steam and will recondense on cool surfaces such as the window.

Activity 2: Evaporation
A saucer of water left by an open window or on a radiator will evaporate.

You can set this up for initial observation. Then challenge the children to devise experiments to test conditions for evaporation. For example, does evaporation occur quicker in a draught, in the open air, on a day when the air pressure is high, or in warm or cold rooms.

They will need to test these conditions by measuring the same amount of water out each time, and then checking their experiment every hour or so for change in water level.

Mention to the children that when they see their breath on cold mornings it is the warm water vapour from their mouths that condenses on the cold air to create the 'cloud' they see.

Activity 4: Human safety and hot liquids
Tell the children that different solids become liquid and then gas at different temperatures. Warn them of the dangers of this, as boiling water scalds human skin. Cooking oil has a higher boiling-point, and hot oil is therefore very dangerous indeed. There are possibilities for drama or puppet work here to produce a 'safety at home' video for the younger children in the school to watch.

Activity 5: Molecular activity
Discuss with the children what is happening at a molecular level: that all molecules in all things are in motion with kinetic energy. The molecules in solids move less than they do in liquids. When heat energy hits molecules, it is changed to kinetic energy and the molecules move even faster, sometimes sufficiently fast to cause a solid to change into a liquid (e.g. warmed ice turns to water), or a liquid into a gas.

Activity 6: Solids, liquids, gas game
The children can also play a solids, liquids, gases game, where one child thinks of a solid, liquid or gas and the others have to ask questions about its properties in order to identify it. The child being questioned can only answer 'yes' or 'no'.

Copymaster 56 gives the children the chance to link what they know about solids, liquids and gases to their uses.

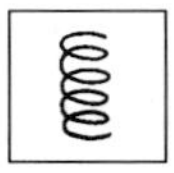

Area of study 12 | P of S 2c | LD 3

IRREVERSIBLE CHANGE

Purpose
To show that we use chemical reactions to convert, irreversibly, materials into products that are useful to us.

Materials needed
Plasticine® or clay, plaster of Paris, Fimo® or other play dough; cake ingredients, mixing tools, cake cases and tins, the use of the school oven; films or videos about glass and plastic manufacture; metal objects showing signs of rust.

Activity 1: Plaster of Paris
Assemble some moulds that the children have made from clay or Plasticine®, and set them out on newspaper. Make up the plaster of Paris as instructed. Work quickly because it begins to set within minutes. Pour the mixture into the moulds and leave until completely hard before peeling away the Plasticine® or clay. Let the children feel the vessel in which you made up the plaster of Paris. Explain that the warmth they feel is the sign of a chemical reaction taking place, in this case into a hard brittle material. Tell the children that the change is irreversible. Plaster of Paris is used in model making and sculpture, to embellish ceilings and mirror frames and to create a hard bandage case round broken limbs.

Activity 2: Fimo®
Children may have handled Fimo® in *Effects of Heating and Cooling* (Area of Study 9, page 59). Let the children handle either Fimo® or some other soft malleable dough which, when heated in an oven, becomes irreversibly hard and brittle. All potters and some sculptors make use of this change.

Activity 3: Baking powder
Make a batch of fairy cakes using plain flour for half the batch and adding the required amount of baking powder to the other. The results using plain flour should be relatively flat, while those with baking powder in them should rise well. Explain to the children that the addition to the mixture of baking powder (which is a mixture of sodium bicarbonate and cream of tartar) allows a chemical reaction to take place during which a gas (carbon dioxide) is produced which makes the cakes rise. Here is a suggested recipe:

Caster sugar 110 g
Margarine 110 g
2 beaten eggs
Plain flour 175 g
A little water if necessary
1 level teaspoon baking powder

Cream the sugar and margarine together. Beat in the egg. Divide this mixture into two bowls. To the first add half the flour and a little water if necessary to make a dropping consistency. To the second add half the flour well mixed with the baking powder. Add water as

necessary. Spoon the mixture into cake cases in patty tins. Cook at 180°C for 15–20 minutes. The overall yield will be 14–20 cakes, and even the flat ones should be edible!

Activity 4: Glass making and plastic manufacture
Borrow a film or video which shows the process by which glass is made from, among other constituents, sand. Thus from materials of limited use we create the stuff of which our windows, doors, spectacles, drinks containers and a host of other things are made.

Look also at films about the making of various plastics to discover which involve chemical reactions among constituents in order to make products which can be used, for example, for insulation material, packaging, sheeting.

If the school is near a glass or plastics factory, or some other plant where chemical change produces useful products, ask if a manager can come along and tell the children about the manufacturing process involved.

Contact the local Higher Education Institution and ask if they have an Economic Understanding and Industrial Awareness Unit or Centre. People involved in such a Centre should be able to offer you further help and advice.

Activity 5: Looking for rust
Let the children look for rust. Some things they may look at include the following:

- The bodywork on a car that is some years old
- A bike
- Door hinges, railings and other metal parts on the outside of the school buildings.

They need to locate where the rust occurs most. Discuss their findings, and explain that iron needs oxygen from the air and moisture to rust. The change taking place when iron rusts is not reversible. We prevent that process by excluding the air and water from the surface of the metal with a 'coating' like chrome or paint. The children will have seen what happens when the surface coating becomes chipped or flakes off.

Area of study 13 | P of S 2e | LD 4

THE WATER CYCLE

C57

Purpose
To explain the water cycle.

Materials needed
Children's reference books on water; thick card, two circular templates, paper-fasteners, scissors, saucers, graduated cylinders, water.

Activity 1: The water cycle
Explain to the children, and research with them in the appropriate books, the water cycle and its circularity. It includes the following steps: water in rivers reaching the sea; air warmed over land rises drawing in 'wind' over the sea which picks up water vapour; water vapour in air carried over land, warmed by land and then rises. It then cools and water vapour condenses and falls as rain, rain runs into the ground and re-emerges as a spring; the spring trickle becomes a stream and then a river, the river runs down to the sea. The children can record this on a water cycle wheel.

The children can construct their own wheels using the instructions given on copymaster 57.

Activity 2: Evaporation and condensation
The children can demonstrate these by putting a small quantity of water into a container with a wide top, such as a washing-up bowl, and enclosing the bowl in a tent made from clear polythene, complete with a central pole made from, say, a bean stick in a pot of soil. This will need to be rigged on a bench near a window where it will receive direct sunlight. The water in the bowl will evaporate and condense on the polythene. The condensed water can be collected at the edge of the polythene tent. This is a form of water 'still' similar to apparatus used to distil liquids. Some children may like to find out more about such devices in relation to survival in desert conditions.

Area of study 14 | P of S 2f | LD 4

CHANGE THROUGH BURNING

Purpose
To learn that when materials are burned they change, and the changes are not reversible.

Materials needed
Advertising brochures about gas, electric and solid fuel fires; a camping stove, saucepan, milk, mugs, spoons, drinking chocolate and a box of matches; a candle in a holder.

Activity 1: Fires
Collect some advertising brochures about gas, electric and solid-fuel fires. Talk to the children about the kind of fire they have at home and how it operates. Remind them of the dangers of fire. Discuss how the fuel is burned to produce heat and waste gases which escape via a chimney or flue. The chimney is necessary both to allow a flow of air which the fire needs to burn and also to evacuate dangerous gases from the home. The fuel once burned cannot be reclaimed.

Activity 2: Camping stove
Place a camping stove at a safe distance from the children. Explain that the compressed gas inside is burned to release the heat necessary to cook on, and that waste gases escape into the air. Make the children a hot drink! Explain that we cannot change the 'fire' back into the gas that was in the stove.

Activity 3: Matches
Look at the way a match works. The starter fuel at the tip is ignited, the wooden stick burns, giving out heat, and waste gases escape. Remind the children of the dangers of matches. Show the children the carbon that is left when the wood burns. Explain that, once burned the match cannot be recovered.

Activity 4: Burning a candle
Light the candle and explain to the children that the solid wax melts to a liquid which, when hot, becomes gaseous and burns, giving off light, heat and smoke. This is an irreversible change. The candle cannot be retrieved once burned.

Activity 5: Burning needs oxygen
Light a candle and set it safely upright in a holder. Invert a glass jar over it and watch the candle go out because of a lack of a supply of oxygen from the air. Do observe safety regulations in doing this experiment.

Activity 6: Excluding oxygen to put out a fire
Invite a local fire-fighter to visit the school and discuss why foam is used in fire extinguishers to put out fires.

Programme of study: Materials and their properties

3. Separating mixtures and materials

Pupils should be taught:

a that solid particles of different sizes, *e.g. those in soils,* can be separated by sieving;

b that some solids, *e.g. salt, sugar,* dissolve in water to give solutions but some, *e.g. sand, chalk,* do not;

c that insoluble solids can be separated from liquids by filtering;

d that solids that have dissolved can be recovered by evaporating the liquid from the solution;

e that there is a limit to the mass of solid that can dissolve in a given amount of water, and that this limit is different for different solids.

Area of study	P of S	LD
15	3a	2

USING A SIEVE

Purpose
To learn the purpose of a sieve, to separate a mixture.

Materials needed
A garden sieve, plastic kitchen sieves and toy sieves used for sand play; garden soil and a beach sand sample; gloves.

Activity 1: Sieving
Unless the sample of soil or sand is known to be clean the children should wear gloves for this activity.

Ask them to experiment with the sieves to see what happens to the soil sample. When they have tried using sieves with holes of a variety of sizes, ask them to work systematically as follows:

- Take a beaker or jug of soil that has not been sieved.
- Set out three sieves, one with large holes, one with medium holes and one with small holes.
- Seive the soil through these in turn.
- Tip the sample left in each sieve on to white paper.
- Number the samples.
- Examine and talk about what is in the samples.

Area of study 16 | P of S 3b, c | LD 4

SOLUBILITY AND FILTRATION

C58

Purpose
To understand what is meant by solubility and filtration.

Materials needed
Salt, sugar, instant coffee, washing powder, sand, wood shavings, grated carrot (or other vegetable); glass or plastic beakers, spoons, water and timers with second hands, Celsius thermometers, filter papers and funnels.

Activity 1: Solubility in water at room temperature
Let the children attempt to dissolve a spoonful of salt, sugar, instant coffee, washing powder, sand, wood shavings and grated carrot in different beakers of water. If they work in pairs they cannot only determine which of these materials dissolves, but also how long it takes to do so. They will need a timer with a second hand for this.

Activity 2: Solubility in hot water
Ask the children to predict what will happen to the solubility of soluble materials as the temperature of the water increases. They can repeat Activity 1, but this time they also need to record the temperature of the water. Then supply them with some warmer water and ask them to repeat the experiment. Finally, give them really hot water to repeat the experiment again. Their results should show increased solubility at higher temperatures.

Discuss with the children the use we make of the fact that some solids are soluble in liquids, for example washing powder.

Copymaster 58 is intended for the children's record of these results.

Activity 3: Filtration
Ask the children to suggest ways in which insoluble solids can be removed from a solution. A coarse sieve would work for large particles.

Show them what filter paper looks like and how it is used.

Allow the children to filter one of the solutions containing insoluble particles produced in Activity 1.

Area of study 17 | P of S 2c, d | LD 5

SEPARATING AND PURIFYING A MIXTURE

Purpose
To explain and implement various techniques for separating and purifying mixtures.

Materials needed
Sand, salt, iron filings, beakers, a funnel, filter-paper and a magnet covered in paper; several different inks or black felt-tip pens; blotting paper.

Activity 1: Separating a mixture of sand, salt and iron filings
Give the children the dry mixture and challenge them to separate out the three things. They may decide to add water right away to dissolve the salt. Then they can filter off the salt solution, dry the filter paper, draw off the iron filings with the covered magnet and set them aside (make sure the magnet is covered or the iron filings will be stuck there forever). The sand can be shaken off the dry filter-paper. If the salt solution is left to evaporate, the salt will be left in the beaker. Alternatively, the iron filings can be drawn off with the magnet right at the beginning of the experiment if water has not yet been added at that stage.

Activity 2: Purification
Discuss with the children the implications of their experiment in Activity 1 for the processes involved in purifying drinking water and sewage and cleaning swimming pools.

Activity 3: 'Who dun it?'
This one is for fun! Out of sight of the children, write a note of confession about a bogus crime, (see the example on the next page). Use a sample of black ink or a black felt-tip, and blot it with blotting paper, making sure there are substantial blots of ink. Create a number of imaginary characters who may have committed the crime (rather like the people in the game of Cludeo®). Assign each character a different black ink or felt-tip pen. Let the children mark strips of blotting paper with the inks and set the strips into jars with a little water in them, so that the inky end dips into the water. Anchor each strip to the side of the jar using a peg so that the strip does not flop right down inside the jar. The constituent colours in the inks should separate up the blotting strips, and only one will match the colour array that can be obtained from the blots made by the ink used in writing the confession note.

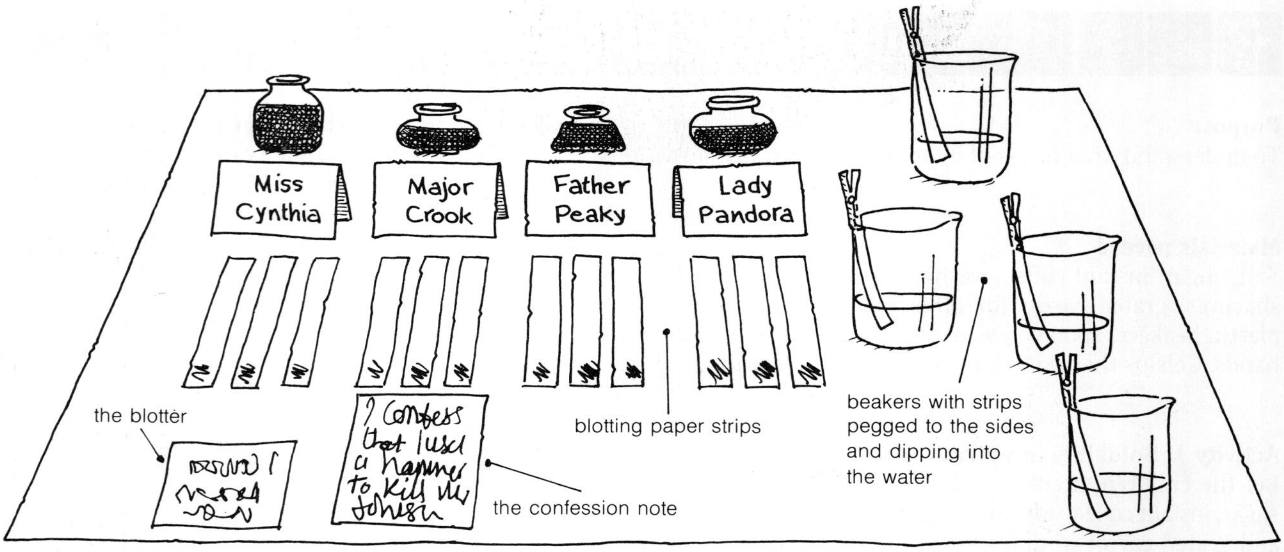

Area of study 18 | P of S 3e | LD 5

MAKING A SATURATED SOLUTION

Purpose
To make a saturated solution.

Materials needed
Transparent beaker measuring jug, water, sugar, accurate balance, spoon, bath salts, salt.

Activity 1: Sugar solution
Show the children how to measure 200 ml water into the beaker. Ask them to add 1 g of sugar at a time, stirring each time. They should continue adding and stirring until the sugar fails to dissolve. The solution is then **saturated**.

Activity 2: Comparing saturated solutions
Ask the children to make up saturated solutions of: bath salts, sugar and salt (carefully weighing the amount of solid required each time and using the same volume of water each time). Discuss the difference in the mass of solid required for different solutions.

Physical processes

How the Areas of study in this book relate to the section of the Programme of study and Attainment target level descriptions. Programme of study			Areas of study and 'best fit' with Level descriptions			
			Level description 2	**Level description 3**	**Level description 4**	**Level description 5**
1. Electricity		Pupils should be taught:				
simple circuits	**a**	that a complete circuit, including a battery or power supply, is needed to make electrical devices work;		Area of study: 1	Areas of study: 2, 3	
	b	how switches can be used to control electrical devices;		Area of study: 1	Areas of study: 2, 3	Areas of study: 4, 5
	c	ways of varying the current in a circuit to make bulbs brighter or dimmer;				Areas of study: 6, 7
	d	how to represent series circuits by drawings and diagrams, and how to construct series circuits on the basis of drawings and diagrams.				Area of study: 7
2. Forces and motion						
types of force	**a**	that there are forces of attraction and repulsion between magnets, and forces of attraction between magnets and magnetic materials;	Area of study: 8	Area of study: 9		
	b	that objects have weight because of the gravitational attraction between them and the Earth;			Area of study: 10	
	c	about friction, including air resistance, as a force which slows moving objects;			Area of study: 11	
	d	that when springs and elastic bands are stretched they exert a force on whatever is stretching them;			Area of study: 12	

Physical processes

How the Areas of study in this book relate to the section of the Programme of study and Attainment target level descriptions.			Areas of study and 'best fit' with Level descriptions			
Programme of study			**Level description 2**	**Level description 3**	**Level description 4**	**Level description 5**
		Pupils should be taught:				
	e	that when springs are compressed they exert a force on whatever is compressing them;			Area of study: 12	
balanced and unbalanced forces	**f**	that forces act in particular directions;	Areas of study: 13, 14, 15			Areas of study: 20, 21
	g	that forces acting on an object can balance, *e.g. in a tug of war, on a floating object, and that when this happens an object at rest stays still;*	Areas of study: 13, 14, 15			Area of study:21
	h	that unbalanced forces can make things speed up, *e.g. an apple being dropped,* slow down, *e.g. a shoe sliding across the floor,* or change direction, *e.g. a ball being hit by a bat.*		Areas of study: 16, 17	Areas of study: 18, 19	Areas of study: 20, 21
3. Forces and motion						
everyday effects of life	**a**	that light travels from a source;	Area of study: 22			
	b	that light cannot pass through some materials, and that this leads to the formation of shadows;			Areas of study: 24, 25	
	c	that light is reflected from surfaces, *e.g. mirrors, polished metals;*		Areas of study: 23	Areas of study: 25	Areas of study: 26, 27
seeing	**d**	that we see light sources, *e.g. light bulbs, candles,* because light from them enters our eyes;			Area of study: 28	Area of study: 29

Physical processes

How the Areas of study in this book relate to the section of the Programme of study and Attainment target level descriptions.			Areas of study and 'best fit' with Level descriptions			
Programme of study			**Level description 2**	**Level description 3**	**Level description 4**	**Level description 5**
		Pupils should be taught:				
vibration and sound	**e**	that sounds are made when objects, *e.g. strings on musical instruments*, vibrate but that vibrations are not always directly visible;	Area of study: 30			Area of study: 35
	f	that the pitch and loudness of sounds produced by some vibrating objects, *e.g. a drum skin, a plucked string*, can be changed;	Area of study: 30			Areas of study: 35, 36
	g	that vibrations from sound sources can travel through a variety of materials, *e.g. metals, wood, glass, air*, to the ear;	Area of study: 31		Areas of study: 32, 33, 34	
4. The Earth and beyond						
the Sun, Earth and Moon	**a**	that the Sun, Earth and Moon are approximately spherical;	Area of study: 37			
periodic changes	**b**	that the position of the Sun appears to change during the day, and how shadows change as this happens;			Area of study: 38	
	c	that the Earth spins around its own axis, and how day and night are related to this spin;				Areas of study: 39, 40
	d	that the Earth orbits the Sun once each year, and that the Moon takes approximately 28 days to orbit the Earth.				Areas of study: 41, 42, 43

Level descriptions: Physical processes

Level descriptions

Level 2

Pupils know about a range of physical phenomena and recognise and describe similarities and differences associated with them. They compare the way in which devices, such as bulbs, work in different electrical circuits. They compare the effects of similar phenomena, such as the brightness or colour of lights, or the loudness or pitch of sounds. They compare the movement of different objects in terms of speed or direction.

Level 3

Pupils use their knowledge and understanding to link cause and effect in simple explanations of physical phenomena, such as a bulb failing to light because of a break in an electrical circuit, or the direction or speed of movement of an object changing because of a force applied to it. They begin to make simple generalisations about physical phenomena, such as explaining that sounds they hear become fainter the further they are from the source.

Level 4

Pupils demonstrate knowledge and understanding of aspects of Physical processes drawn from the Key Stage 2 or Key Stage 3 Programme of Study. They describe and explain physical phenomena, such as how a particular device in an electrical circuit may be switched on or off, or how the apparent position of the Sun changes over the course of a day. They make generalisations about physical phenomena, such as motion being affected by forces, including gravitational attraction, magnetic attraction and friction, or sounds being heard through a variety of materials. They use the idea that light travels to explain phenomena such as the formation of shadows.

Level 5

Pupils demonstrate an increasing knowledge and understanding of aspects of Physical processes drawn from the Key Stage or Key Stage 3 Programme of Study. They begin to apply ideas about physical processes to suggest a variety of ways to make changes, such as altering the current in a circuit or altering the pitch or loudness of a sound. They begin to use some abstract ideas in descriptions, such as forces being balanced when an object is stationary, or objects being seen when light from them enters the eye. They use models to explain effects that are caused by the movement of the Earth, such as the length of a day or year.

Programme of study: Physical processes

The relationship between forces and motion should be made clear. It should also be made clear that both light and vibrations from sound sources travel from the source to a detector. Work on the Earth's place in the solar system should be related to pupils' knowledge about light.

1. Electricity

simple circuits

Pupils should be taught:

a that a complete circuit, including a battery or power supply, is needed to make electrical devices work;

b how switches can be used to control electrical devices;

c ways of varying the current in a circuit to make bulbs brighter or dimmer;

d how to represent series circuits by drawings and diagrams, and how to construct series circuits on the basis of drawings and diagrams.

Area of study 1 | P of S 1a, b | LD 3

ELECTRICAL CIRCUITS

C59

Purpose
To demonstrate that a complete circuit is necessary for electrical appliances to work.

Materials needed
Covered wire suitable for electrical circuit-making, wire cutters, a lamp and lamp-holder, a cuboid battery of the same voltage as the lamp, press-on terminals, a buzzer, balsa wood, drawing pins, paper clip.

Activity 1: Creating a circuit
Connect the lamp to the battery. Point out to the children some of the important words and ideas, including the fact that terminals need to be clean, the wire clean and bare at the connections (i.e. uninsulated), and that a good contact must be maintained at all connections. When the circuit is complete, the lamp lights up. Show the children what happens if you disconnect the circuit at any point.

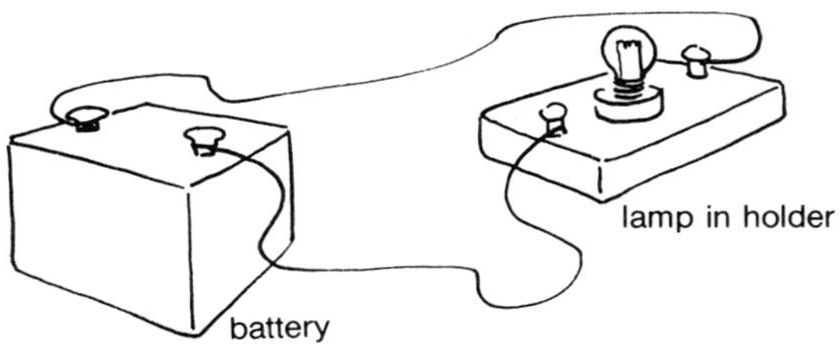

Activity 2: A buzzer circuit
Connect the lamp to the battery as in Activity 1. Take an additional piece of wire and connect a buzzer into the circuit. Show the children what happens when the circuit is broken.

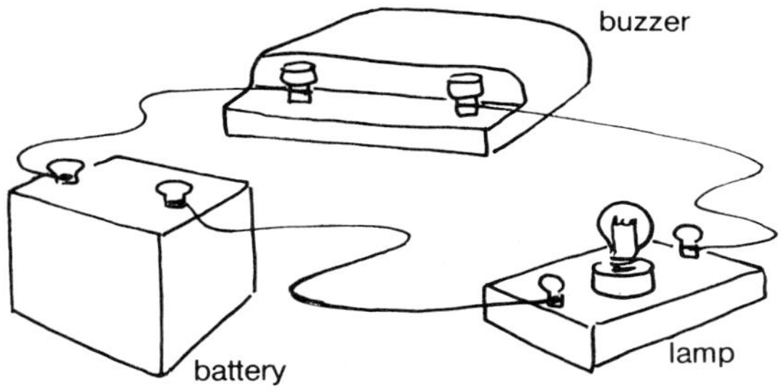

Activity 3: Switches
Ask the children what happens in a light circuit when you operate the switch. Make a switch as shown. Put the switch into a circuit similar to the one created in Activity 2. Let the children have a go!

A home-made switch

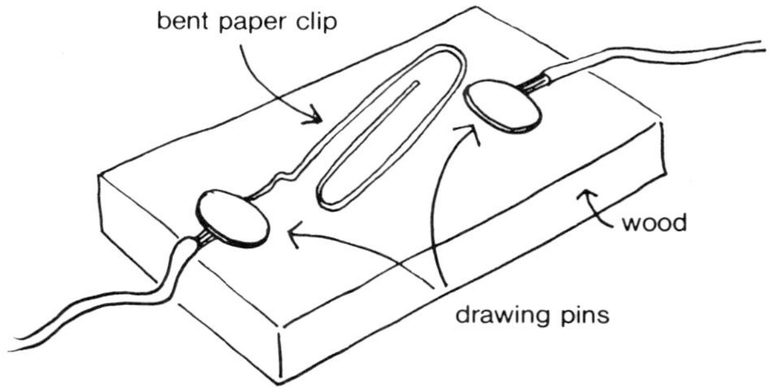

Activity 4: Fuses
A fuse in a circuit is a safety device to stop too much power entering and breaking equipment. If the maximum current for the fuse is exceeded the fuse blows breaking the circuit. Show the children the kind of fuse found in the fuse box at home, and take apart a disconnected electric plug to show them the fuse in it. Fuses can vary according to the maximum current they can carry. Tell the children that they should ON NO ACCOUNT touch the fuses or tamper with plugs at home.

Create a display of all the things used in the demonstration circuits, and then let the children handle them.

Copymaster 59 can be used to check that the children understand the necessity for a complete circuit for a flow of electricity.

Area of study 2 | P of S 1a, b | LD 4

CIRCUIT CONSTRUCTION

C60

Purpose
To be able to make an electrical circuit.

Materials needed
Quantities of wire suitable for circuit-making, wire cutters, a variety of batteries; lamps in lamp-holders, buzzers and switches (or materials for making these, including wood blocks, drawing pins, paper clips or metal strips); press-on terminals and crocodile clips.

Activity 1: Rules of circuit-making
Remind the children of the need for clean terminals, bare wire at connections, good connections, a compatibility of power source and appliance and the need for a complete circuit without breaks. Make up a circuit containing a battery and lamp. Disconnect this circuit and give the children a chance to make their own circuit.

Activity 2: Buzzers and switches
Provide the children with a wide variety of circuit-making equipment and let them experiment in finding circuits that work.

They can record their efforts on copymaster 60.

Activity 3: Circuits in model-making
Let the children make shoe-box models such as a shop, room, disco or football stadium. They can then create a circuit for lighting it appropriately.

The models will make a stunning impact at a parents' evening display.

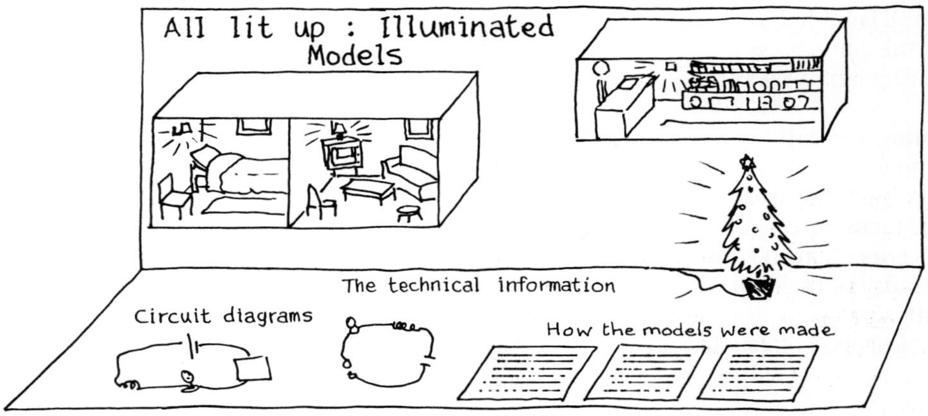

Area of study 3 | P of S 1a, b | LD 4

MORSE

C61

Purpose
To explain that Morse employs electrical circuits and to send and interpret Morse messages.

Materials needed
Reference information about Morse, including a Morse alphabet; wire suitable for circuit-making, wire cutters, batteries and lamps, switches.

Activity: Morse messages
Let the children create a circuit with a power source, lamp and switch in it. Using the switch they can send a short Morse message to a friend, who can then use the equipment to reply.

Copymaster 61 can be used to record this experiment.

Area of study 4 | P of S 1b | LD 5

SWITCHES AND RELAYS

C62, 63

Purpose
To demonstrate how to use switches and relays in simple circuits.

Materials needed
Batteries, bulbs, thin copper wire (obtainable from old transformers), paper clips, drawing pins, plastic covered wire, examples of commercial switches and relays, flexible metal strips (smooth), metal clips, large nails, electric bells/buzzers, bimetallic strip, electronic sensors.

Activity 1: Switches
Give the children a collection of materials such as flexible metal strips, drawing pins, paper clips, etc. and invite them to design and make two kinds of switches:

a) switches that go on or off when released,
b) switches that slide on/off and remain in position.

Test for ease of use, durability, overall construction and ease of connection in a simple circuit.

The children can draw the kinds of switches they produce on copymaster 62.

Activity 2: Electromagnets
Get the children to make a simple electromagnet by winding thin copper wire round a large nail and connecting the ends of the wire to a battery and a switch to complete a circuit. You will need to experiment to find out how many times the wire needs to be wound round to create an electromagnet.

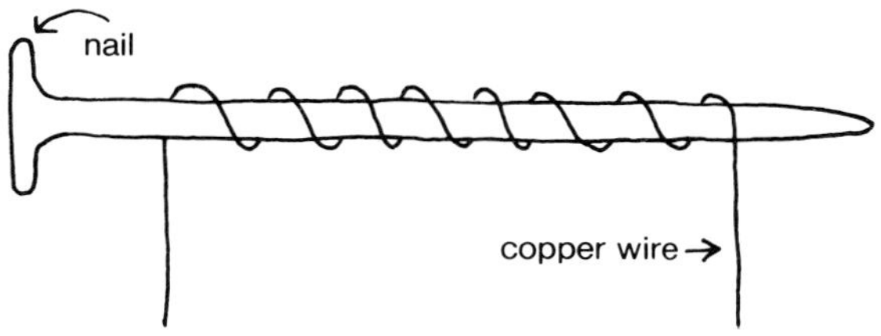

Try picking up small metallic objects. Release them by using the switch. Discuss where such devices might be useful, e.g. picking up cars or scrap metal, and then examine electric bells and buzzers.

Electric bells and buzzers work through the use of electromagnets which are rapidly switched on and off by the movement of the flexible arm which makes and breaks the electrical contact (see diagram opposite). 'Make and break' switches are part of the range of switches children need to be aware of. Some children could attempt to make their own buzzers using iron bolts, flexible metal strips, etc.

Activity 3: Bimetallic strips and thermostats
Demonstrate the effect of applying heat to a bimetallic strip. These strips are formed by the bonding together of two metals which have different expansion rates. Heat will cause the strip to bend as one metal expands more rapidly than the other. Get children to collect data about the existence of temperature controllers (thermostats) in their homes. Examples can be found in kettles, fires, irons and central heating controllers.

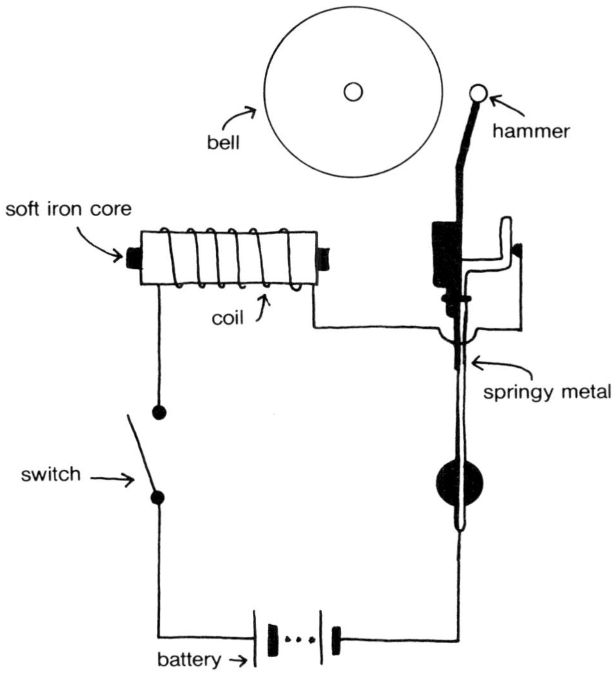

Copymaster 63 can be used to record information about thermostats at home.

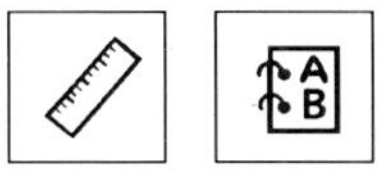

Activity 4: Sensors
If you have light sensors or other sensors available try out some simple detection circuits with the children. Ask the children to seek out the use of sensors in everyday life, e.g. shop-lifting detector barriers, burglar and fire alarms, counting devices and sound sensitive devices. Make a group list of all the items that the children discover,

Area of study 5 | P of S 1b | LD 5

LOGIC GATES

C64

Purpose
To explain logic gates in decision-making and control circuits.

Materials needed
Circuit symbols, dice and counters.

Activity 1: Decisions
The children will be familiar with tables and decision-making trees from their work in Mathematics. To understand logic gates it is useful to build on this knowledge by posing some 'dilemmas' which can be analysed in terms of the number of options open to them. For example, the answer to the question 'Can I go swimming?' might have two embedded questions:

a) Have I enough money?
b) Am I free at the right time?

If the answer to a) is NO then it is not possible to go even if the answer to b) is YES. All of the possible answers can be laid out in the form of a table.

Have I enough money?	Am I free at the right time?	Can I go swimming?
NO	NO	NO
YES	NO	NO
NO	YES	NO
YES	YES	YES

In only one case is it possible to go swimming, and that is where the answers to the questions are Yes to (a) **AND**

Yes to (b). This is a **TRUTH TABLE** and is an example of an **AND** situation. In an **AND** gate it is necessary to have two inputs in order to get an output.

Give the children some examples of this sort of decision-making.

Another sort of truth table can be constructed in answer to a question such as 'Do I need to wear my fur-lined boots?' You will need your boots if it is cold or raining.

The table looks like this:

Is it cold?	Is it raining?	Do I need to wear my fur lined boots?
NO	NO	NO
YES	NO	YES
NO	YES	YES
YES	YES	YES

There is only one possible occasion when you *do not* need your boots. In this case, the table is produced on the basis of whether one **OR** the other question is answered in the positive. With an **OR** gate either of the two inputs produces the output.

Give the children some examples of this sort of decision-making.

The final logic gate is a **NOT** gate. This is rather different from the other two in that it has only one input and it acts, apparently, rather strangely. If there is a positive input then there is no output. If there is no input there is an output.

Play the logic gates game on copymaster 64.

Activity 2: Logic gates in use

Try to get the children to consider examples of where they meet or hear about logic gates being used, e.g. frost warning devices, some burglar alarms, some car alarms, cameras with warnings for light levels and washing machines.

The children can try designing some simple circuits. For example, a simple car alarm which would sound if the door was opened would be an example of an **AND** circuit. A simplified diagram is shown here.

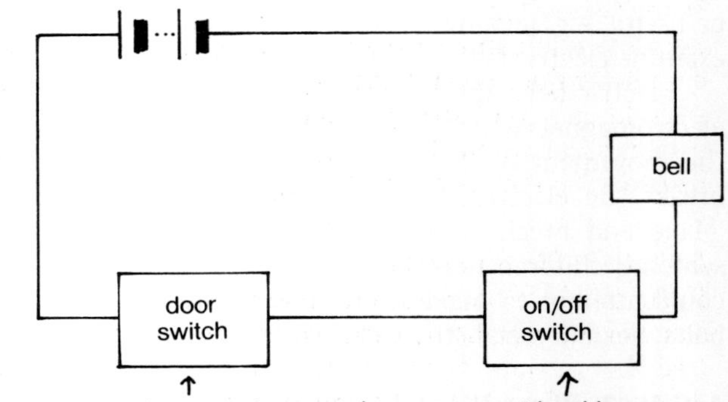

Area of study 6 | P of S 1c | LD 5 | VARYING THE FLOW OF ELECTRICITY | C65, 66

Purpose

To vary the flow of electricity in circuits and note the effects.

Materials needed

Radio, simple electric model railway with controller, leaflets and booklets about household lighting switches and controllers, a rheostat (variable resistor), battery, compatible bulbs in bulb holders, switches, circuit wire, wire cutters, fuses and fuse wire.

Activity 1: Variable resistors in everyday life

Put the radio on and demonstrate the use of the volume control. To reduce the level of sound, the control offers more resistance to the current. ('Resistance' is how well a material resists electricity flowing through it.) See if the children can think of other controls which operate like this.

Dimmer switches for lighting operate in the same way, as do the controls in some cars which dim the lights on the instrument panel.

Activity 2: Model railway controller

Set up a simple loop of track and set the train going. Use the controller to vary the speed of the train. Let the children time how long the train takes to go round the track 10 times, with the controller set at various positions. Start the timing after the train has started moving at an even speed.

The children can record their results on copymaster 65.

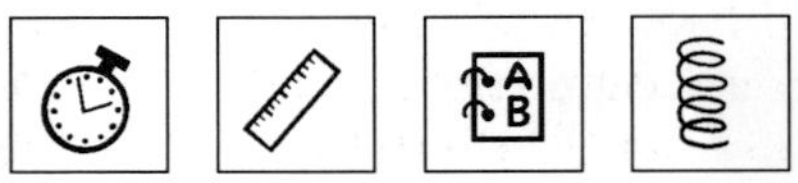

Activity 3: Inserting a variable resistor in a circuit

Let the children construct a simple circuit with a battery, switch and bulb. Put a variable resistor, of the rheostat type, into the circuit. Move the control on the resistor and observe the brightness of the light bulb. Discuss with the children the length of resistance wire the current is passing through when the control is in various positions. Look at samples of fuse wire and compare the thicknesses with the maximum current that can be carried.

This experiment can be recorded on copymaster 66.

Area of study 7	P of S 1c, d	LD 5	CIRCUIT CONSTRUCTION	C67, 68

Purpose
To connect power sources and equipment in series and parallel, to draw these circuits using symbols, and observe and explain the outcomes.

Materials needed
Booklets that come with electrical appliances, wire for circuit-making, several batteries of the same size and strength, several lamps in holders compatible with the batteries, press-on terminals, crocodile clips, bells, resistors, ammeters and voltmeters.

Activity 1: Circuit symbols
If the children have not met them already, give them some of the commonly used symbols in circuit-making (see the diagram opposite). Let them look for circuit diagrams in booklets that come with electrical appliances such as radios and record players. They can see which circuit symbols they can interpret.

Copymaster 67 comprises a list of symbols.

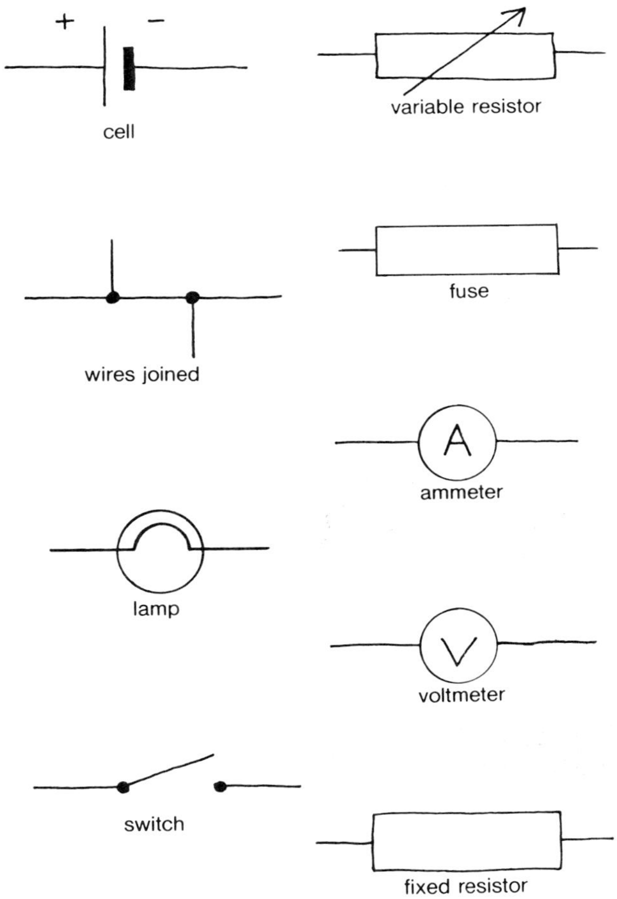

Activity 2: Circuits in series: more batteries
The children should be familiar enough with circuits in series to be able to make a simple circuit of lamp and power source, and then add other batteries in series. If you have an ammeter, introduce this into the circuit and the children can measure the current.

Activity 3: Circuits in series: more lamps
Add lamps in series to a simple lamp and power source circuit. The children should note that each additional lamp makes all the lamps become dimmer.

Activity 4: Circuits in parallel: more batteries
Ask the children if they can add more batteries to a simple lamp and power source circuit, so that the lamp does not look brighter, but all batteries are contributing to light the lamp. They should connect the batteries in parallel. An ammeter will show the current in the circuit. They should find the current constant and the lamp of constant brightness however many batteries are in the circuit.

Activity 5: Circuits in parallel: more lamps
If the children now put more lamps in parallel, each lamp should be as bright as if there were only one bulb, but the battery power will expire quicker because the battery power is shared.

All these experiments can be recorded on a worksheet such as copymaster 68, though the children may need more than one copy.

Activity 6: Designing a circuit
Ask the children to design a circuit, and then get a friend to make it up using the circuit diagram. They can see if their friend can do it without help, and whether the circuit does what was intended.

Programme of study: Physical processes

1. Forces and motion

Pupils should be taught:

types of force

a that there are forces of attraction and repulsion between magnets, and forces of attraction between magnets and magnetic materials;

b that objects have weight because of the gravitational attraction between them and the Earth;

c about friction, including air resistance, as a force which slows moving objects;

d that when springs and elastic bands are stretched they exert a force on whatever is stretching them;

e that when springs are compressed they exert a force on whatever is compressing them;

Area of study 8 | P of S 2a | LD 2

MAGNETS ATTRACT SOME MATERIALS

C69

Purpose
To show that magnets attract some materials and not others.

Materials needed
A collection of small pieces of various materials, including paper, a candle, brass, a can, steel, iron, glass, cork, rubber, plastic and wood; objects such as paper clips, drawing pins, buttons (brass, other metal and plastic); bar, horseshoe and circular magnets.

Activity 1: What does a magnet attract?
Arrange a display of magnets and small items made of a variety of materials. Let the children experiment to find out what is attracted to the magnet. When the materials have been sorted into two sets, the children can suggest what is similar about all those things which are attracted to the magnet. They will note that all the things the magnet has attracted are metal, but that not all metal objects are attracted to it. Tell them that iron has to be present for attraction to occur.

The children will want to experiment on objects around the room and on buttons, eyelets, jewellery and other things they are wearing. Tell them that magnets should be kept AWAY from wrist-watches, clocks, cassettes and videos because they can disrupt the working of these.

Activity 2
The children can carry their exploration further by finding out whether magnets still attract through the table, through glass or plastic. They can also begin to experiment with the strength of magnets by seeing how many paper clips each of a variety of magnets will pick up.

The children can consolidate work on magnetic attraction on copymaster 69.

123=

Area of study 9 | P of S 2a | LD 3

MAGNETIC NORTH AND SOUTH

C70

Purpose
To explain the Earth's magnetic field, and the fact that magnets can repel one another.

Materials needed
Bar magnet, a clamp on a stand, string, chalk, a pocket compass.

Activity 1: Magnetic north and south
Tie a piece of string around the magnet and suspend it from the clamp so that it can swing freely. If it is difficult to balance the magnet, make a pipe-cleaner cradle for it. The magnet will come to rest lying in a north-south direction. Lay a piece of paper under the magnet. Draw a chalk line to mark exactly how the magnet was at rest. Move the suspended magnet right away and show the children a pocket compass. They may know what it is and what it is used for. You can show the children that if you align the pointer in a north-south direction it should match the direction of 'lie' of the suspended magnet. Tell the children that the earth is like an enormous magnet. If we allow a small magnet to move around, it will line up with the earth's magnetic north and south. Let the children take a compass outside the classroom and also into the playground. Then discuss with them the constancy of north.

Activity 2: Using a compass
Lay out a map, preferably of the area surrounding the school. It should have a geographic north printed on it. If you set the compass down on the map, the children should be able to turn the map so that north on the map corresponds to north on the compass. This is just how walkers, orienteers and other travellers work out their route.

Use copymaster 70 for children to record which is north on a 'map' of the classroom. They will need help with this.

Activity 3: Magnets can repel each other
Suspend a bar magnet as in Activity 1, and bring one end of another bar magnet near to one end of it. One end of the hand-held magnet will attract, the other will repel the pole of the hanging magnet. Tell the children that like poles repel one another. See if you can buy some small magnetic toys. These can be made to swivel away from one another.

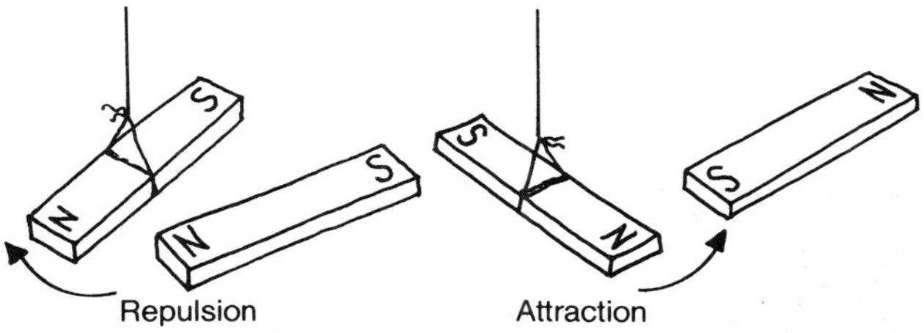

Area of study 10 | P of S 2b | LD 4

GRAVITATIONAL FORCE AND WEIGHT

C71, 72

Purpose
To explain that falling objects are subject to a force of attraction towards the centre of the Earth; that it is the effect of gravity on mass which gives objects weight; and that we measure the force of weight in newtons.

Materials needed
Pictures of astronauts in space capsules and on the Moon, a video of astronauts moving in spacecraft; a collection of objects which you may drop safely from a height, including sticks and wood blocks, pebbles and leaves, bits of plastic, paper and card; a stairwell or window two floors up from which to drop these objects and a timer appropriate for this activity (see note in Activity 2); string, weights, clamps, protractors, second timers.

Activity 1: Gravitational force
Children know that if they drop something it falls to the ground, and if they jump, they come down again. Tell them that there is a force pulling things on the Earth towards its centre and this is called gravitational force. Because the force affects everything, the weight of things is a combined measure of mass and gravitational force and is measured in newtons. The children can speculate about what would happen if gravitational force was reduced. Show the children film of space travel.

Activity 2: What happens when we drop things
This activity needs careful setting up and supervision by a teacher. The things do need to be dropped from a height, and it will depend on your school where the most appropriate place is. If you are using a stairwell, the well will have to be guarded so that no one enters it while the experiment is in progress. Similarly the ground below a high window will need a 'no-go' barrier to minimise danger to anyone underneath. The children can then drop a collection of objects. They can determine what factors influence the speed, motion and direction of fall. These will include shape and size.

Finding an appropriate timer for this task with children working at this level is a problem. Galileo used his own pulse: it may be possible to try this with the children.

Copymaster 71 can be used to record results of dropping experiments done by the children.

Activity 3: Pendula investigations
Let the children set up a pendulum by hanging a small weight from a length of string and suspending it from a clamp. They can time the 'swing', and determine how many swings there are to a minute. Ask them to guess what might happen if the length of the pendulum, the weight on it or the starting arc are changed. Let the children test out their ideas.

Results can be recorded on copymaster 72.

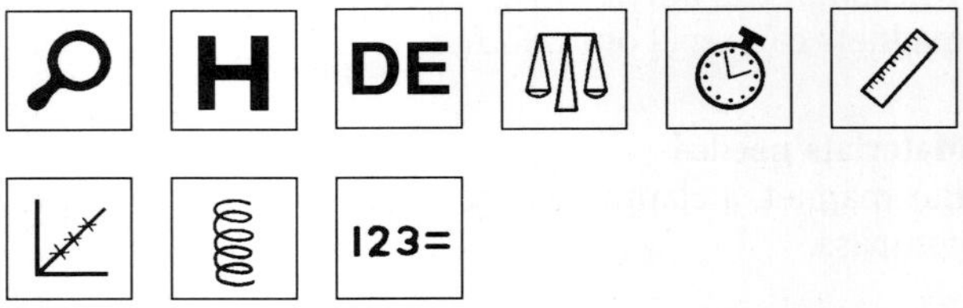

Area of study 11 | P of S 2c | LD 4

FRICTION AND AIR RESISTANCE

C73

Purpose
To describe the effects of friction, and to explore air resistance.

Materials needed
A pencil rubber, water, cooking oil, a smooth surface; a block of wood, various materials to change the surface of a table, e.g. waxed paper, fabric, sheet plastic, sandpaper, string, masses; scissors, paper, Plasticine®, paper clips; information about the latest bicycles.

Activity 1
Discuss what the children understand by the term friction, and how we experience it every day in, for example, moving about, the stopping distance on a bicycle or in a vehicle, using matches and playing stringed instruments.

Activity 2: Vehicle tyres and friction
Replicate tyres by using an old pencil rubber, pressing it along a dry, wet and oily surface.

Activity 3: Friction investigation
Put a wood block with a string and a mass in a bag attached to it on to a variety of surfaces. Allow the string and bag to hang over a table edge. Add masses to the bag until the block starts to move.

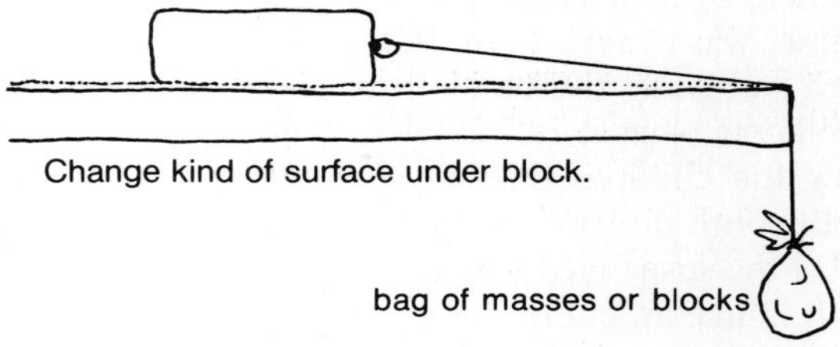

The mass necessary to start the block moving on each of the surfaces can be recorded on copymaster 73.

Discuss with the children the effects of the surface on the mass necessary to start the block moving.

Activity 4: Paper aeroplanes
Invite the children to make paper aeroplanes and trial them. They could design a plane, make it, fly it, and after evaluation modify the construction. Inspect and discuss the planes and tell the children they will go faster if they are more 'stream-lined' (that is allow air to flow over them easier).

After the children have constructed their improved aeroplanes, conduct speed tests. Mark a start and finish line, and time the planes over that distance.

Activity 5: Bicycles and air resistance
Olympic-standard cyclists are using bicycles and helmets specially designed to reduce air resistance and allow high speeds. Look at some of these designs and compare them with ordinary bicycles and helmets.

Area of study 12 | P of S 2d, e | LD 4

SPRING AND ELASTIC BAND FORCE

C74

Purpose
To show that stretched springs and elastic bands exert force.

Materials needed
Cotton reels, rubber-bands, spent matches, card, sticks (such as plant-support sticks), beads, long pins with

stout heads, balsa wood, craft knives, short nails and a hammer, a long balloon, a round balloon, nylon fishing line, plastic drinking straws, sticky tape, Lego®; toys and other objects using springs.

Activity 1: Rubber-band force: cotton reel toy
With a cotton reel, a rubber-band and two spent matches the children can make a rubber-band-powered toy. Reduce friction on one end of the cotton reel by rubbing it with a candle. Anchor the band at the other end of the cotton reel through the centre of the reel with a short length of matchstick. Push a longer matchstick into the rubber-band at the waxed side of the reel and twist until quite tight. Try out how many turns are necessary to make it move, not over- or under-winding. Make sure one end of the longer match extends beyond the rim of the reel, so that it touches the ground. Set down the reel and it should move. If you have difficulties it may help to have a smooth bead through which the rubber-band is passed at the driving end. Once the children have got their models moving effectively, they can experiment to see whether more turns of the band means the toy travels a greater distance. They can try and make it climb a ramp, too.

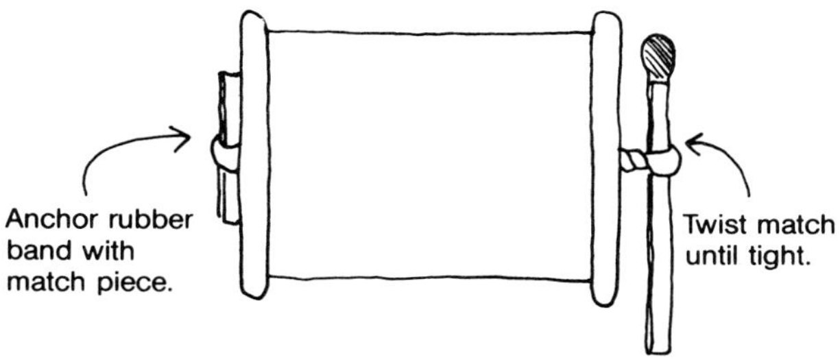

Activity 2: Rubber-band force: paddle-boat
Let the children make a paddle-boat out of balsa wood, as shown below. (The paddle may be made from balsa wood or thick card.)

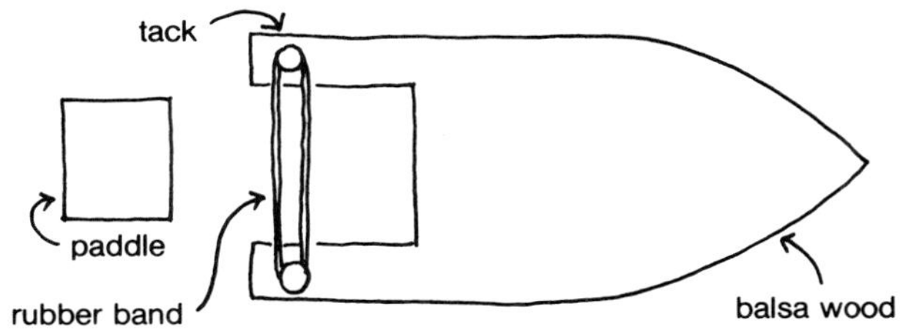

Let the children try out their boats in water. Can they predict what will happen if they wind the band the other way?

Copymaster 74 can be used for the children to record how they made their boats and how test 'sailings' went.

Activity 2: Stretching and compressing springs
Collect together a variety of items that have springs as part of their mechanism. Examples include: suction toys with springs attached that pop up; toys that dangle and bounce from a spring; clockwork toys where a spring inside is wound tight and released; desk lamps. Show these to the children and discuss how they work, and whether the spring is stretched or compressed in each case. Explain that the **force** of the spring will make the toy move.

Programme of study: Physical processes

2. Forces and motion

balanced and unbalanced

Pupils should be taught:

f that forces act in particular directions;

g that forces acting on an object can balance, *e.g. in a tug of war, on a floating object,* and that when this happens an object at rest stays still;

h that unbalanced forces can make things speed up, *e.g. an apple being dropped,* slow down, *e.g. a shoe sliding across the floor,* or change direction, *e.g. a ball being hit by a bat.*

Area of study 13 | P of S 2f, h | LD 2

PUSH AND PULL IN SPORTS AND GAMES

C75

Purpose
To show that human pushes and pulls make things start to move, go faster, swerve and stop in sports and games.

Materials needed
Equipment used in a variety of games and sports, including, e.g. roller boots, skateboard, ice-skates, skipping-ropes, football, table tennis bat, a bicycle, sledge, a video of snippets of various sports in action, or a range of sports pictures, a smooth board and some coins for 'shove ha'penny', marbles, coffee jar lids and round cheese box lids, and models and toys with wheels.

Activity 1: Push and pull in active sport
Let the children examine and discuss a range of items used in active sport, and talk about where the pushes and pulls occur and what it is that moves in a rugby scrum, in a kick-off, on a bicycle or on roller boots, for example. Let the children try out or use school equipment to help them to determine where they are pushing and pulling, and what it is that moves. Create a display of sports items and pictures of sports in action. The children can add their own labelled drawings of people playing sport, marking in the push and pull and movement.

Copymaster 75 can be used by the children for work on the idea of human muscle power giving the push and pull in sport. There are complex ideas here, and human movements are not always simple enough to carry a straightforward 'push' or 'pull' label. Discuss this with the children to clarify their thinking.

H

Activity 2: Pull and push demonstrations
Let each child practise skipping using a rope. They can skip and determine when they are pulling, when they are pushing and what moves as a result of those forces.

Activity 3: Push and pull with games and toys
A 'shove ha'penny' board is ideal for showing push. Create one on a polished wood or plastic worktop surface (e.g. Formica®), with spaces marked on it as shown (see below). Place this flat on the table.

A coin is placed so that it slightly overlaps the starting edge of the board. The children apply force ('shove') directly to the coin with the flat or heel of the hand to get it to move. The aim of the game is to get three coins in each of the nine spaces on the board. To have a turn you shove five coins.

Toys on wheels, including Lego® models, toy cars, prams and pushchairs all give children the chance to apply direct force in moving something, accelerating it, swerving it and stopping it. If the children trap some marbles under the lid of a jar, they have an experimental toy that responds very well to push and pull.

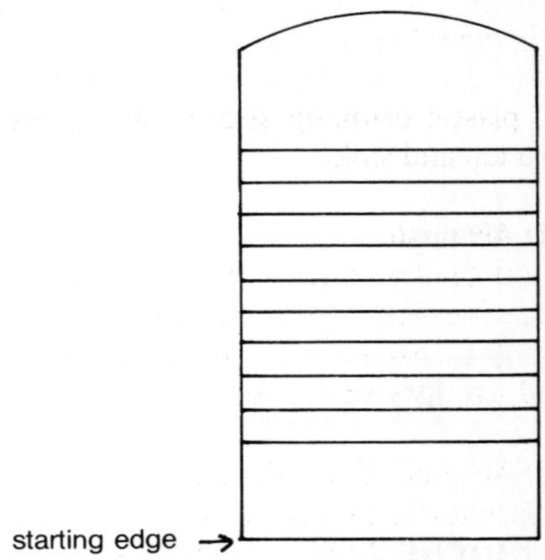

Area of study 14 | P of S 2f | LD 2

PUSH AND PULL IN USE OF TOOLS

C76

Purpose
To demonstrate that human push and pull can operate hand tools.

Materials needed
Wood offcuts, large nails, a hammer, a saw, a hoist (like that available with some washing-lines) or clothes' airer; wire coat-hanger, cotton reel, plastic straw, weight, piece of string. These are the minimum tools necessary, but ideally every child should have a chance to experiment with a range of tools, under adult guidance and supervision.

Activity 1: Force in using a hammer
Bang in a nail. This uses push. Human force, applied through the hammer has made the nail move.

Activity 2: Force in using a saw
In closely supervised conditions let the children saw through a piece of wood. Let them determine whether they are applying as much force on the pull as the push stroke.

Activity 3: Pulleys
Ask the children to look for pulleys in use on building sites. Demonstrate the use of a pulley in helping human force using a washing-line hoist or a clothes' airer. Let the children try it out. Then help the children make a single fixed pulley by first cutting the straight part off a wire coat-hanger. Insert the cut ends through a cotton reel which has a length of plastic straw inserted through the centre. Suspend the pulley and dangle a weight on a piece of string over the reel. Heave-ho! Human pull is doing the work. Does the pulley make pulling more comfortable? A simple pulley does not give mechanical advantage, but does make work more convenient.

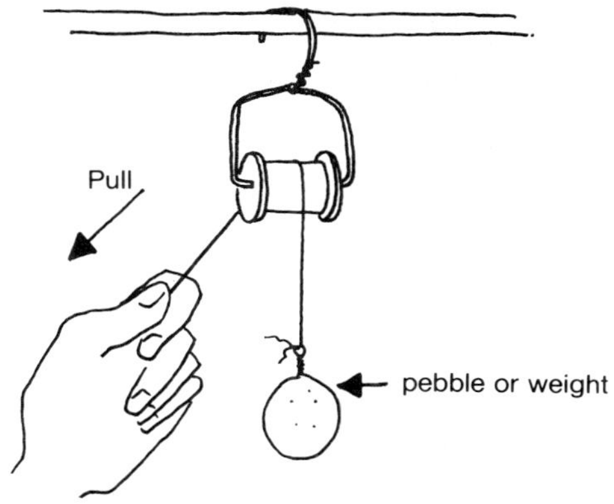

Use copymaster 76 for the children to indicate whether a range of hand tools use push or pull forces.

H

Area of study 15 | P of S 2f, h | LD 2

AIR AND WATER PUSH AND PULL

Purpose
To show that liquids and gases can exert force and that we make use of these forces.

Materials needed
Pictures of a hydroelectric power station, windmills, windsock, windvane and signs above shops and on garage forecourts; a model sailboat and a blow football set. Pictures of and information about watermills, a toy water-wheel, an empty drinks can, pieces of balsa wood and card, plastic drinking straws, strong model glue. Access to a tap and sink.

Activity 1: Air push
Look at a range of pictures with the children, including windmills, windsocks, windvanes and hanging and free-standing signs. Discuss what happens to these in light breeze and strong wind.

Activity 2: Air push and sailboats
A small sailboat in a sink can be made to move and turn by creating a 'wind'. A piece of card flapped up and down will create a breeze, or the children can blow on the sail. They can determine what it is about the force ('wind') that affects the boat. Speed and direction are two factors involved. They can experiment with card pieces and tubes and drinking straws to change the direction and 'force' of the blow.

Activity 3: Blow football
Play the game and discuss the direction of the push given by the air and the direction of subsequent movement of the ball.

Activity 4: Uses of water force
Look at the working of a watermill. The water 'push' on the wheel turns the machinery in the mill to grind the corn.

Show pictures of a hydroelectric power station and explain briefly that it is the force of the flowing water that is used to make electricity.

Activity 5: To show water force
You may have a water-wheel bought for sand and water play. If so, the children can find out what makes it go round quicker. Is it more water, or the distance the water falls on to the wheel?

Make a water-wheel from an empty drinks can with stiff card flaps stuck to it. Give the wheel a pencil or plastic straw axle and suspend it under a running tap. Make sure the sink cannot be plugged! Let the children see what happens when just a trickle of water falls on the wheel, and then when the tap is turned on full.

Area of study 16 | P of S 2h | LD 3

FORCE AND MOVEMENT

C77, 78

Purpose
To demonstrate that when things start to move or stop moving, forces are acting on them.

Materials needed
A bicycle with good brakes, toys with wheels, ramps; paper of several kinds (including tissue, copy, typing and cartridge paper) for making paper aeroplanes.

Activity 1: 'Start and stop' play with cars
Let the children establish as many ways as they can of starting and stopping the motion of a simple toy car. They will find they can start it moving by pushing it or putting it on a ramp, and it can be stopped by an obstruction or using an 'escape road' with a soft surface such as sand. Encourage them to vary the force applied by asking: Does the car travel further if you push harder? Are there other things we can do to make it travel further?

The children can record their activities on copymaster 77.

Activity 2: 'Start' play with paper aeroplanes
Make some paper aeroplanes. There are several books currently available to help you with a simple design.

By playing with the aeroplanes, the children should identify important factors in flight: size and direction of force applied, and size, shape and material used in construction. See also Area of study 11, Activity 4.

The children can follow the instructions on copymaster 78 and make their own aeroplanes.

Activity 3: Stopping force
Let the children examine and draw the working of bicycle brakes. The brake pads are pressed with force on to the bike rims. Get them to check what happens when only a little force is applied to the brakes, and to find out why using just front brakes is not a good idea. This work can be tied in with cycle safety, by predicting what happens if the brake pads are worn.

Area of study 17 | P of S 2h | LD 4

MOVEMENT AND FORCES

C79

Purpose
To show that how much an object moves can depend on the size and direction of the wind force on it.

Materials needed
Card, paper fasteners, sticks (such as plant-support sticks), craft knives, a round balloon, a plastic straw, sticky tape, nylon fishing line.

Activity 1: Wind force: windmill
Let the children make paper or thin card windmills as shown at the top of the next page.

The details of this construction have been set out on copymaster 79 so that the children can make it for themselves.

Test out the windmills by blowing or applying wind from a hairdryer, to see whether the direction and force of the wind make a difference to the motion of the windmill.

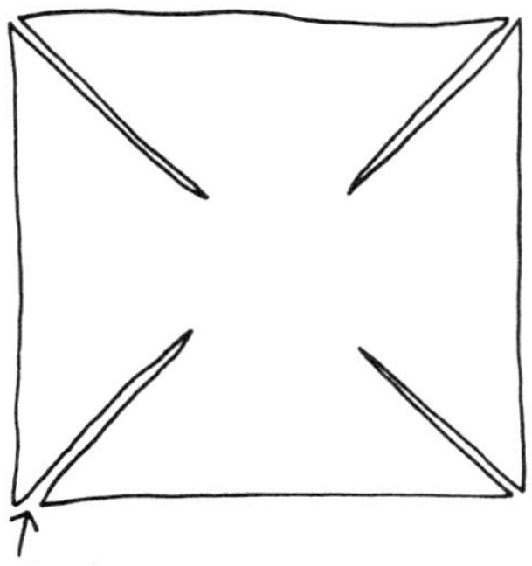

Cut from corners.

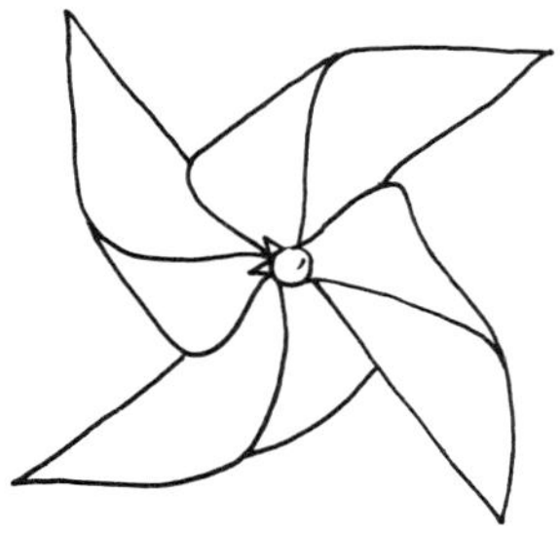

Fold into centre and push paper fastener through.

Activity 2: Wind force: balloon rocket
Attach one end of a length of nylon fishing line at one side of the room. Blow up a long balloon and keep the air in it by putting a clothes peg on the open end. Stick a plastic drinking straw to the balloon lengthwise with sticky tape. Pass the free end of the line through the straw, and ask a child to hold the line so that it is just taut. Move the balloon so that it is near the child's hand. Stand clear of line. Countdown! Release the peg. The children should (when they stop laughing) be able to say what makes the rocket go. Let them experiment to see if the wind power will take the rocket up a sloping line.

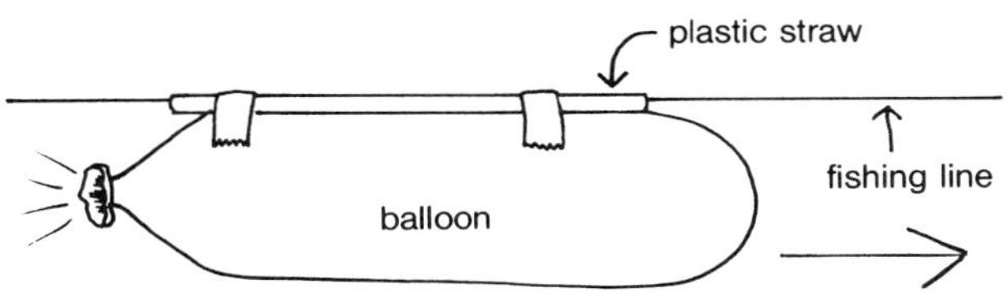

Activity 3: Wind force: go-kart
Encourage the children to make a small Lego® trolley. Inflate a balloon and pinch the neck together with a peg, making sure that there is enough neck to grip. Fix this end over the end of a piece of bendy plastic straw and seal the balloon on to the straw with sticky tape. Stick the balloon to the kart with tape. Release the peg and away it should go! Ask the children what makes it go.

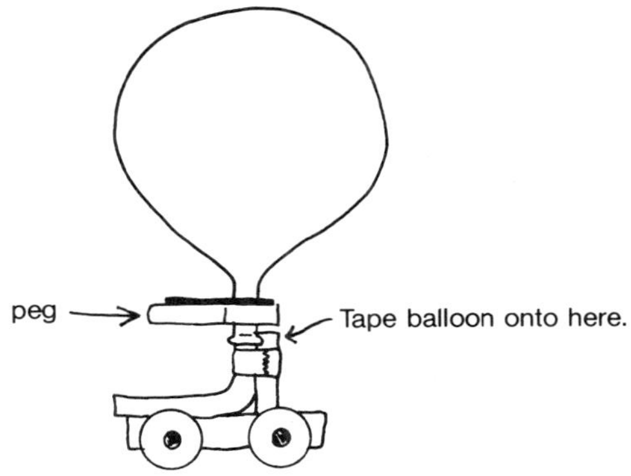

Activity 4: Hydraulics and pneumatics
Discuss the fact that liquids transmit pressure and that this is put to use in the brake systems of many cars, the 'tip-up' mechanisms in trucks and lorries and in mechanical diggers.

Pneumatic systems utilise compressed air or other gases. There are sophisticated construction sets available for children, like Lego® Technics, which enable them to construct working models.

Area of study	P of S	LD
18	2h	4

STOPPING A MOVING OBJECT

C80

Purpose
To demonstrate that the faster an object is moving, the greater the force/time needed to stop it.

Materials needed
Pictures of playground equipment, a baby's spinning top, a gyroscope, toy cars and a long wooden ramp, marbles and plastic track such as curtain track.

Activity 1: Stopping on playground equipment
Look at the pictures of playground equipment, which should include a roundabout, swings and bucking horse. Discuss the relative force or time needed to stop the equipment when it is moving slowly or fast.

Activity 2: Stopping a spinning top
If children play with the top they will see that the faster they make it go before releasing it, the longer it will go before stopping.

Activity 3: Stopping a gyroscope
Demonstrate with the gyroscope that the more turns you give to the string on it and the faster it goes, the longer it spins before stopping.

Activity 4: Speed and stopping distance using toy cars
Set up a long fixed ramp. Let the children put a toy car on it at a marked spot, half-way up the ramp, and mark where the car comes to rest. They can measure the distance travelled. They will need to do this a number of times, reject those where the car swerves, and take the average of the measured distances. They should then put the same car at the top of the ramp, and again, for a number of trials, measure the distance travelled. There is a link here between the speed achieved by the car and its stopping distance.

Activity 5: Speed and distance using marbles
As in Activity 4, let the children release a marble half-

way up a fixed sloping track and record over several trials the distance the marble travels. The same marble can then be placed at the top of the same fixed track and the distance travelled recorded again. The link between speed and distance travelled can be established.

Results of the distances travelled in the trials in Activities 4 or 5 can be recorded on copymaster 80.

Activity 6: Stopping distance and road safety
Ask the local police force if a road safety officer can come to talk to the children specifically about stopping distances (i.e when the steady force of the brake is applied) and their implications for pedestrians, cyclists and everyone using the roads. Ask the police for some statistics about stopping distances and recreate these distances in the playground, getting the children to stand the appropriate distance apart.

Area of study 19 | P of S 2f, h | LD 5

FORCES, DISTANCE AND TIME

C81

Purpose
To explain and to measure forces, distance and time.

Materials needed
A variety of springs and clamps, tins, a water supply, metal strips, a tool kit and vice, marbles, a wooden board, pieces of wood, wood glue, kit to make an electronic timer; long fixed ramp, balloon pump, rubber bands and string, balsa wood, a variety of toy cars and other vehicles, a newton meter; materials to make a trolley, string, masses and hanger, paper strips, washing-up liquid, paint; a pinball toy, part of a snooker game or video.

Activity 1: Making timers
Set up as an open-ended investigation so that the children can explore ways of making timers suitable for measuring different lengths of time. For example, they can set up bouncing springs, water drip tins, vibrating metal strips, rolling ball timers, electronic timer kits.

Activity 2: Stopping force
Let the children set up a long ramp. Attach an inverted balloon pump to the end and fix a thin piece of balsa wood to that. Pull the inner tube out of pump so that it lies ready for pushing. Put each of a variety of vehicles of different mass at the top of the ramp and allow them to bump the pump at the bottom. A chalk mark on the ramp where the pump started, and where it finished, for each vehicle will enable the children to record and talk about a link between mass and stopping force. The experiment can be repeated with vehicles of equal mass but different-sized wheels (Lego® can be used here).

The results of this experiment can be recorded on copymaster 81.

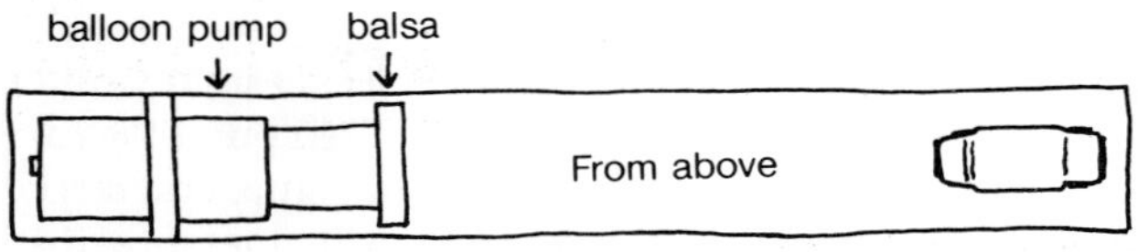

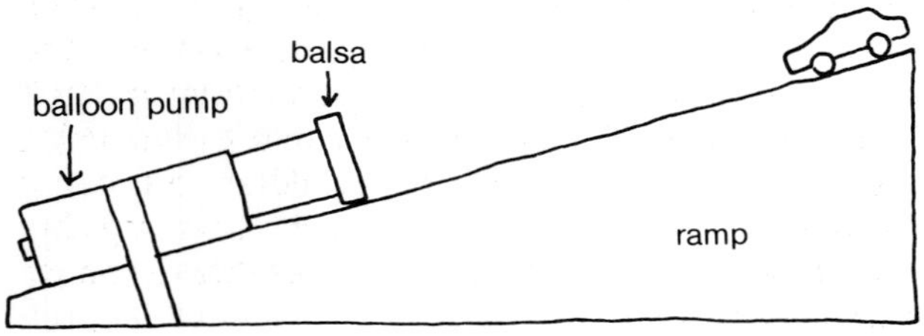

Activity 3: Pulling force
Experiment with a newton meter to determine, for example, the force necessary to open different doors in school.

Activity 4: Force and acceleration link
Construct a trolley from wood, Meccano® or Lego®. (See the diagram at the top of the next page.) Attach a piece of string to the front end of the trolley and allow the string to run over the edge of a table. Attach a bag to the free end of the string. Now fix a strip of paper along the route to be taken by the trolley. Make a drip timer by piercing a hole in an empty can with a drawing pin. Set the trolley down on the strip of paper and tape the can on the back, so that the pinhole is beyond the back of the trolley. Put the trolley at its starting point and add one mass to the bag, but get a child to support the bag until you say 'go'. Pour a little washing-up liquid to which powder paint has been added (paint is slightly more viscous than water) into the timer and let go of the bag. As the trolley runs the length of the table, the timer drips will mark the paper. Catch the trolley before it runs right off the table! Staunch the remaining drips from the timer with a cloth. Do the 'run' several times more, with different coloured liquids and more masses added to the bag.

From the marks on the paper, the children will be able to see that the trolley goes faster when more force is applied to it, for the faster the trolley moves, the fewer the drips.

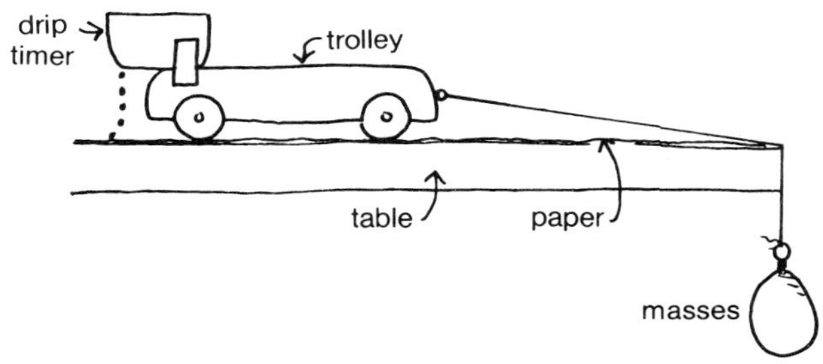

Activity 5: Effect of change in forces on people
To start to understand the idea of balanced forces, talk about what happens when the children are sitting in a car or bus going along at a steady speed. If the vehicle turns or speeds up/slows down suddenly, what happens to them? Can they feel the effect of a change in the forces operating? Tell the children about the principle behind the discussion.

Activity 6: Pinball and snooker
Let the children play with a pinball toy (or a simple game of marbles) and track the routes taken by the balls or marbles.

Watch a video of part of a snooker game, and 'pause' the film each time a ball changes direction, to discuss the direction of the forces on it and the direction of movement. The children can draw some diagrams while the film is held on 'pause'. Top-class players can cause the ball to swerve by making it spin, so some changes of direction for the white (cue) ball will have to be discussed in terms of collision and rotation.

Area of study 20 | P of S 2 f, gh | LD 5

BALANCED FORCES

C82

Purpose
To learn that objects can be acted on by more than one force, and that these forces can be balanced.

Materials needed
A water tank or deep bowl, a collection of objects which can be put into water without them being harmed, including, for example, corks, wood blocks, plastic tubing, crockery, coins, metal bar or ruler, pebbles, fabric, card, paper; fishing floats and weights; plastic bottles, drinks cans, sandwich box, fabric pieces, modelling dough; some things with a low centre of gravity, such as wide-based vases, a ship's decanter, wobbly man and some with a high centre of gravity, such as a stem vase, a table lamp with a flexible stand; cotton.

Activity 1: Finding a set of things that float
Let the children predict from a collection of objects which are those most likely to float. They can give reasons for their thinking. They can then test out their predictions, by putting all the objects in turn into a tank of water. Tell the children that the water appears to be 'holding up' the floating items, and is in fact exerting pressure or force on them. If the density of the object exceeds the density of water then the upthrust is not sufficient to hold it up.

The understanding that water exerts upward pressure and that this is evident in floating objects is important but difficult. The principle is: if the density of the object is greater than that of water, the object will sink despite the upward pressure. If the density of the object is less than that of water, it will displace its own weight of water and then float. The upthrust then equals the weight of the object. Even objects that sink appear to lose weight in water, owing to the upthrust.

Activity 2: To show upthrust
Try this out before doing it with children. Tie a piece of cotton thread to a large stone and try to lift the stone. (See the diagram at the top of the next page.) Take care! The cotton will break. Tie another piece of cotton on to the stone. Place the stone and thread carefully in water. It should be possible to lift the stone in the water using the thread. You can relate this to the children's experience when swimming, i.e. the sense of weightlessness together with the ease with which they can move other swimmers away from them.

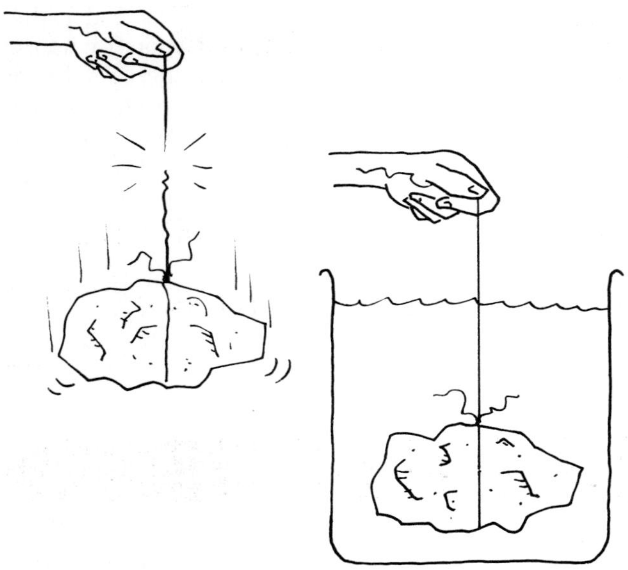

Activity 3: How fishing floats work

Show the children a range of fishing floats. Point out that the fisherman wants to be able to detect a 'bite' by means of the float, so the position it occupies in the water is very important. The weights on some floats are detachable and can be exchanged according to the depth at which you wish them to float. Other kinds of floats have the weights pinched on to the line beneath them and again you can vary the depth of the float in the water by using more or less shot. Make a collection of available floats and weights and the children can see how the weights affect the total density and the amount of float submerged.

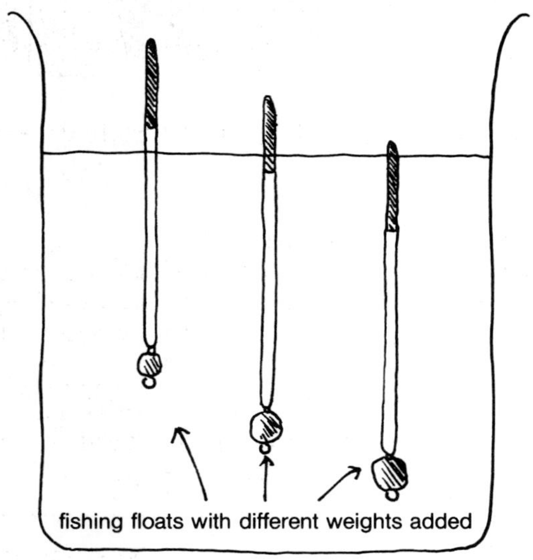

Activity 4: Air-filled things and floating

The children can try putting items such as a plastic fizzy drinks bottle with cap on, a drinks can, a sandwich box with lid, a piece of fabric with holes between the fibres, such as wool, and a small canoe made of modelling dough into the tank. With air in them they will float. When waterlogged or filled with water they will sink. The combination of the material the object is made from and the air is less dense than water. When the material is filled with water, the density exceeds that of water.

The children can record the results of sinking and floating experiments on copymaster 82.

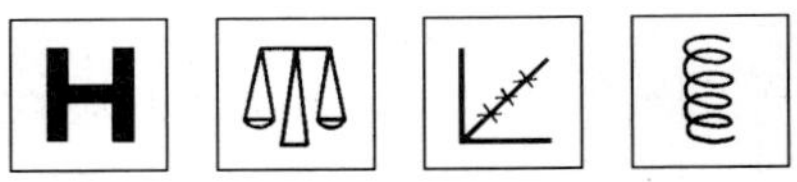

Activity 5: Do floating and sinking rules apply to other liquids?

Carefully place an egg into fresh water. It will sink. Add some salt to the water and the egg will float. Ask the children what they can now say about river water compared with sea water.

Ask the children to try to guess what might happen to boats put into the water. Put small model boats into fresh and salt water samples. What can the children say about how the boats sit in the water? Discuss the idea of Plimsoll lines painted on boats to show the safe load in different waters.

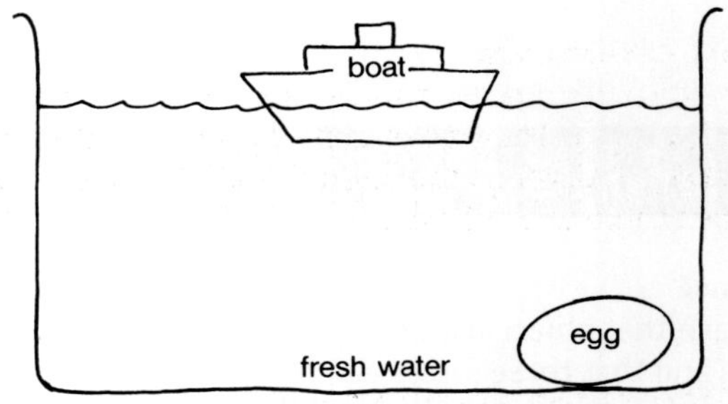

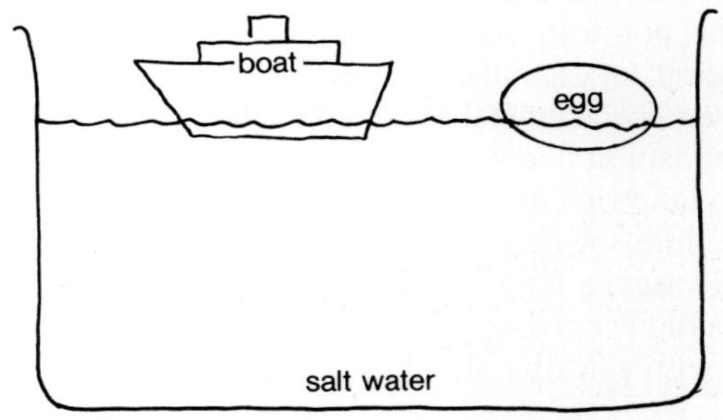

Activity 7: Centre of gravity

Explain to the children that things that are very stable have a low centre of gravity (balance point of the forces upon it). Show them a flower vase with a wide base or a ship's decanter, and a toy that always rights itself. Compare these with a tall vase with narrow stem or top-heavy vase, and a lamp with a flexible stand which will tip over if the lamp head is moved over too far. Discuss the relative stability of, for example, double-decker buses which have a low centre of gravity.

Just for fun let the children cut out the shape of the UK in card. Can they determine the 'centre' and which town lies nearest the centre of the UK?

Programme of study: Physical processes

3. Light and sound

everyday effects of life

Pupils should be taught:

a that light travels from a source;

b that light cannot pass through some materials, and that this leads to the formation of shadows;

c that light is reflected from surfaces, *e.g. mirrors, polished metals.*

Area of study 21 | P of S 3a | LD 2

WHERE LIGHT COMES FROM

Purpose
To understand that light is emitted from a source.

Materials needed
Torches, including a lantern, a pocket torch and a pencil torch; a light box; pictures taken on sunny days and at night.

Activity 1: Torch play
Allow the children to handle torches in a partially darkened room. They can see the beam of light cast by the torch. Tell them the light comes from the light **source** or bulb in the torch.

Activity 2: Light box
Use a light box – the light can be allowed to pass through slits and apertures of varying sizes – to demonstrate that the light beam comes from a source.

Activity 3: The source of daylight
Look at pictures taken during daylight and night-time. Discuss the fact that the Sun is the **source** of daylight. At night we are in darkness or use other light **sources** (for example, electric lights and street lights).

Area of study 22 | P of S 3c | LD 3

LIGHT CAN CHANGE DIRECTION

C83

Purpose
To show that light can change direction.

Materials needed
A collection of reflective surfaces including, e.g. mirrors, lids from take-away meal packs, drinks; glass blocks, prisms, beakers of water. Mirrors, spoons, pans, plain glass and black paper, a tank of water, polished metal; pictures of reflective surfaces including modern buildings, windscreens.

Activity 1: Play with sunlight
Let the children try reflecting sunlight off a wristwatch, a mirror, the surface of a drink and other reflective surfaces on to the wall or ceiling. The light clearly changes direction in going from the reflective surface up to the ceiling. They can also play with glass blocks, prisms and glass beakers filled with water, or a beam of sunlight from a chink in a drawn curtain or blind. In these cases the light changes direction as it passes through the material, and when passed through a prism will give a rainbow effect. This is because white light is broken down into its constituent colours.

Set up a display of things that the children have played with.

Activity 2: Looking for reflections
Let the children look for as many surfaces as possible which allow reflections. Make a display including all they find, and pictures of reflective surfaces which

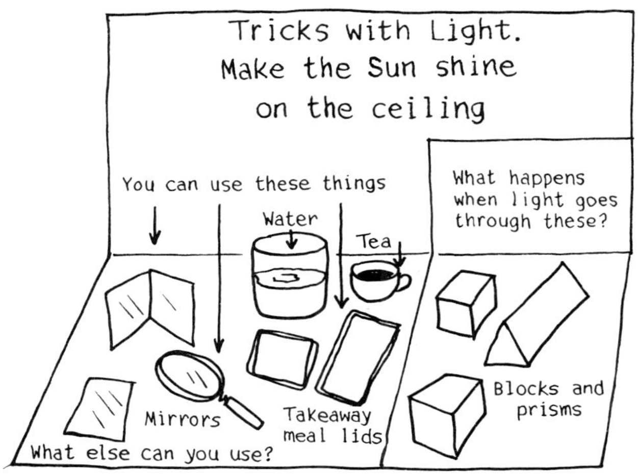

cannot be brought into the classroom, such as modern buildings, puddles and windscreens. Include stories which use reflections in the plot, e.g. *The Ugly Duckling, Chicken Licken* and *Through the Looking Glass*. Discuss the differences in the sizes and shapes of the images they see, and the fact that images are sometimes inverted.

Copymaster 83 can be used to record work on images.

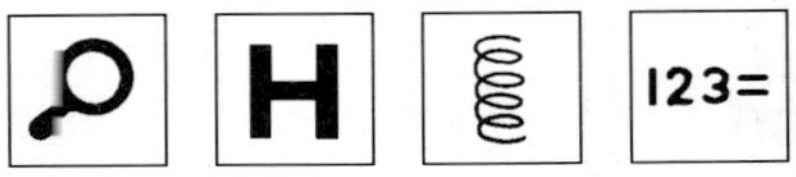

Area of study 23 | P of S 3b | LD 4

SEE-THROUGH AND OPAQUE MATERIALS

C84

Purpose
To show that light goes through some things, and forms shadow when it does not.

Materials needed
Pieces of glass, plastic sheet, coloured cellophane®, sweet wrappers or filters, lenses from old spectacles and sun-glasses, glass blocks and prisms, and containers with water in them; an overhead projector and some opaque objects with distinctive outlines; torches, a sheet screen, shadow puppet making materials, including paper, card, glue, scissors, pea sticks, a craft knife and sticky tape; photographic paper, a black changing bag, sheets of clear, rigid plastic (A4 size), tray of fixer, tray of water.

Activity 1: Seeing through objects
Let the children think of all the things there are that they can see through. Let them play with glass pieces (with protected edges), pieces of plastic, smoked and coloured filters, lenses, glass blocks and prisms and containers with water in them. Tell the children that they can see through all these things because the light we see by comes through them.

Activity 2: Shadow-making 1
Darken the classroom and shine a torch on the wall. Ask a child to stand between the torch and the wall. The children will be able to see the resulting shadow, and suggest why it should occur. The children can try making animal-shaped shadows.

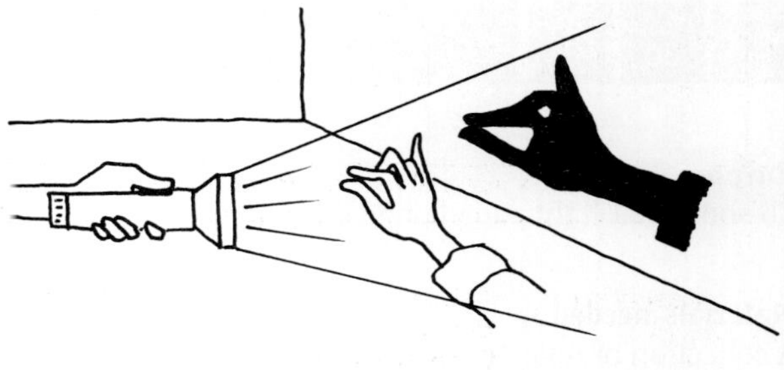

Activity 3: Shadow-making 2
Set up an overhead projector to shine on a screen or wall. Place an everyday object on the projector and its shadow will be projected. Discuss what is happening.

Activity 4: Shadow puppets
Make some shadow puppets from card and paper. Set up a home-made screen from a sheet, as shown at the top of the next page. It is best if the screen slopes forward a little, for the puppets can then be leant against the screen when they are on stage but not moving. Create and perform a show for the whole class, or an assembly.

The children can record their work on shadow puppets on copymaster 84.

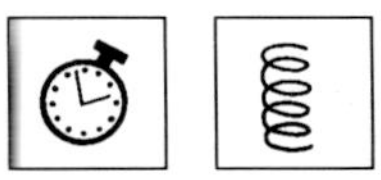

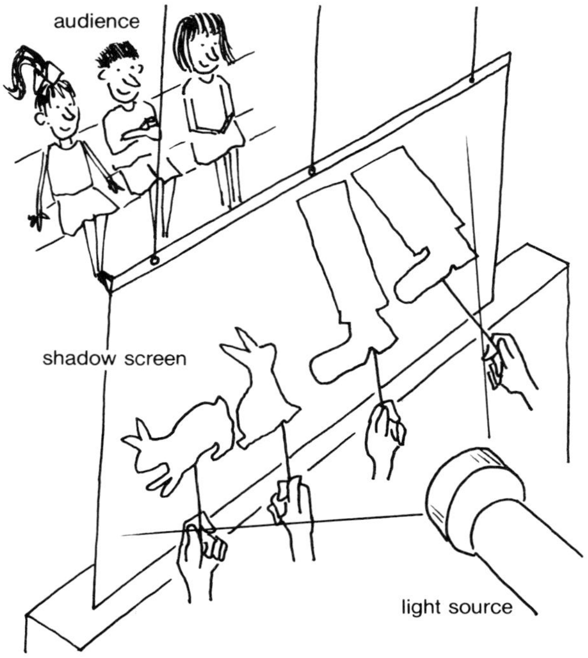

Activity 5: Light-sensitive materials

Put a box of photographic paper into a changing bag, which you can make from light excluding fabric or buy from a photographic dealer. A design for one is shown below.

Let the children lay some shapes like leaves and grasses on an ordinary sheet of paper to make a pattern. Put your hands into the bag and get out a sheet of paper from the box. Close the box. let the children transfer their pattern from the ordinary paper to the sheet of photographic paper. Put a sheet of clear, rigid plastic on top to hold the pattern of leaves and grasses still. Take the photographic paper outside and put in the sunshine until the paper turns a deep colour. This will take from fifteen seconds to thirty minutes depending on the strength of the Sun. Take off the pattern-making materials and submerge the paper in a tray of fixer. Follow the timing instructions that come with the fixer. Put the paper into a tray of water. Wash under running water after the lesson. Leave to dry naturally. The children can produce stunning 'shadow pictures' like this, since the paper lying under the objects remains unexposed.

Pattern for changing bag

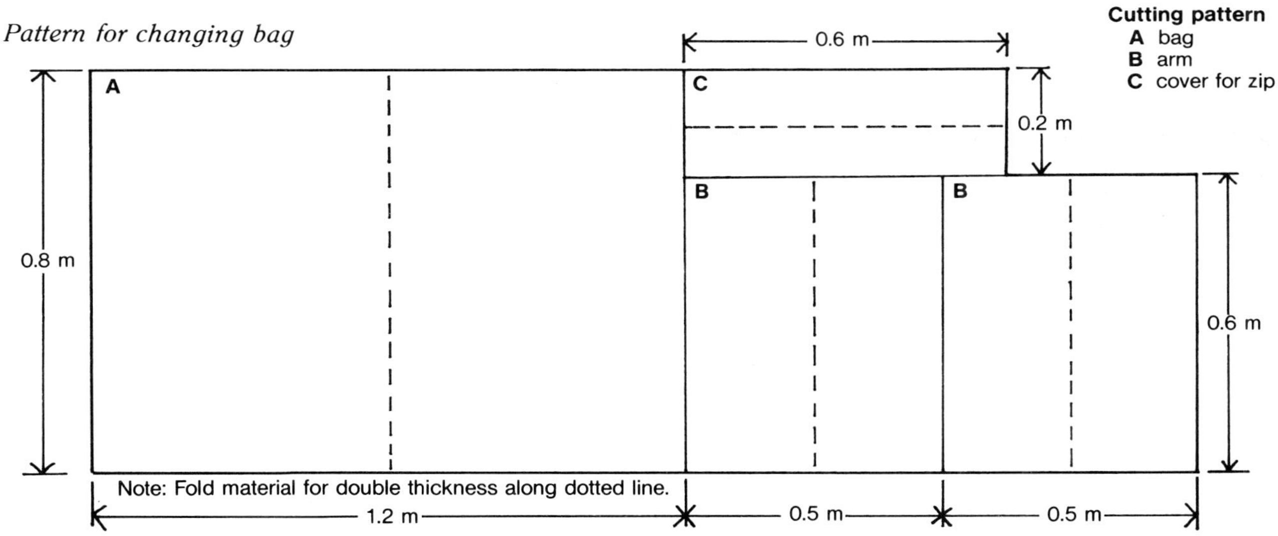

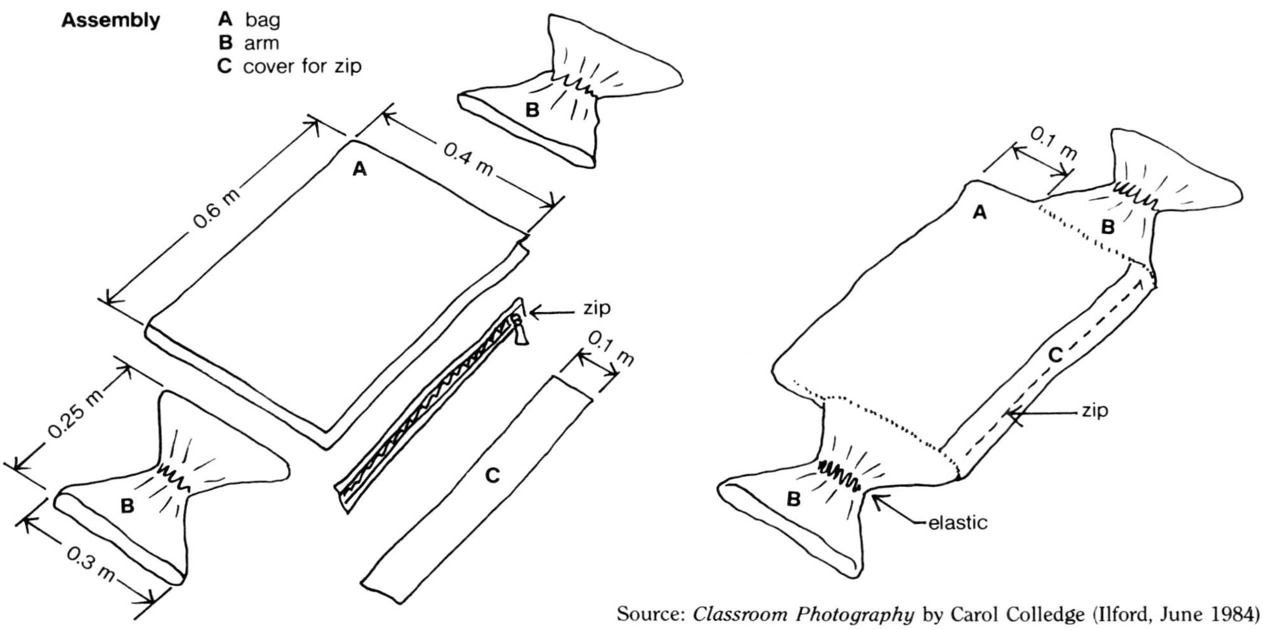

Source: *Classroom Photography* by Carol Colledge (Ilford, June 1984)

Area of study 24 | P of S 3b, c | LD 4

LIGHT TRAVELS IN STRAIGHT LINES

Purpose
To show that light travels in straight lines.

Materials needed
String, pin, pieces of card; chalk, metre stick; torch, cotton, Blu-Tack®, block, paper and pins.

Activity 1: Corner trick
Ask two children to hold either end of a piece of string. Holding the string taut, and looking along the string, let one child take his/her end round a corner of the school building, so that he/she is out of sight. Clearly light does not travel round right angle corners or we should be able to see round them. Ask the unseen child to move slowly towards the corner, holding the string taut all the while. Shout when the child comes just in sight. The string should be a straight line.

Activity 2: Pin-hole trick
Make two small holes in each of a number of pieces of card. Make the holes in the same place and the same distance apart on each card.

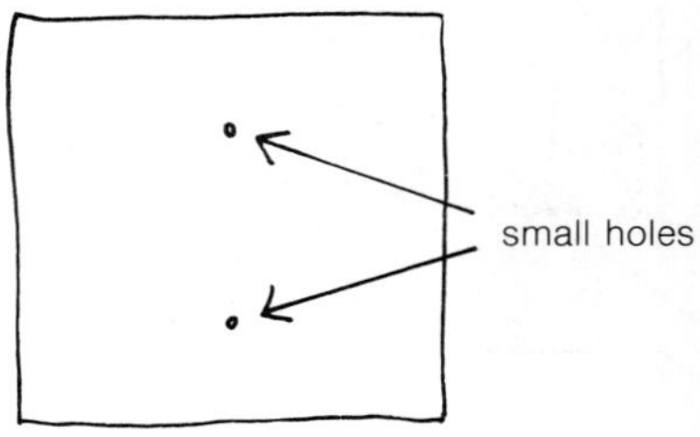

Thread all the cards on to a long piece of string, putting string through the lower hole in each card. Get a child to hold each end of the string, and then station children, one holding each card flat along the length of the string. Ask a child to look along the string through the furthest hole. Then have each pin-hole card put up in turn so that the viewer can see through each one (as below). When they are all up it will be seen that the string, which replicates the viewing line, is straight.

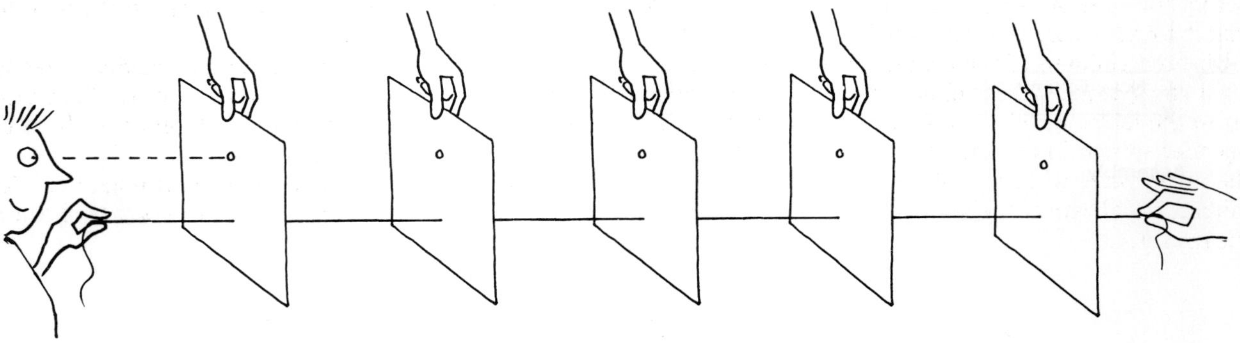

Activity 3: Shadows
If we look at shadows on the playground they are shorter when the Sun is high in the sky and longer when the Sun is lower. If we imagine a straight line drawn from the Sun to touch the edge of our body outline and then pass beyond us on to the ground, it falls at the edge of our shadow. Try out the idea of shadow length being related to the Sun's elevation by letting the children measure shadows in the same spot at different times of day. (Look also at Area of study 40 *The Sun and our year*, page 102.)

Activity 4: Shadow prediction
Stick some lengths of cotton on to the rim of a torch (as yet not switched on). Fix the torch on a block as shown at the top of the next page.

Place a cardboard silhouette near the torch and fix it so that it stands up. Stick the strands of string to the rim of the silhouette with Blu-Tack®, and then take each thread on to a sheet of paper and pin it there so that the cotton has made a straight line from the torch to the paper. From the positions of the pins predict where the shadow will come and draw it in. Switch on the torch.

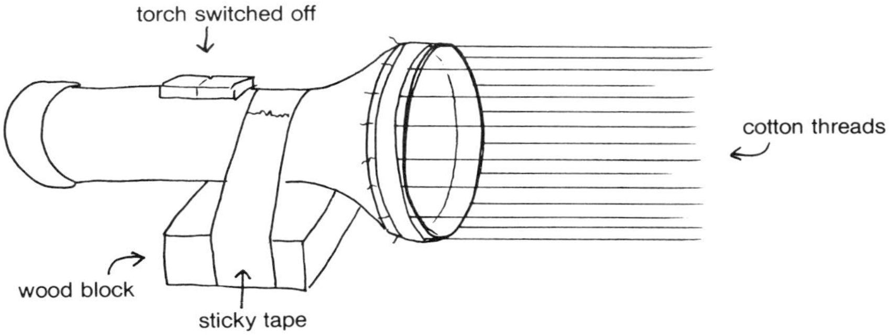

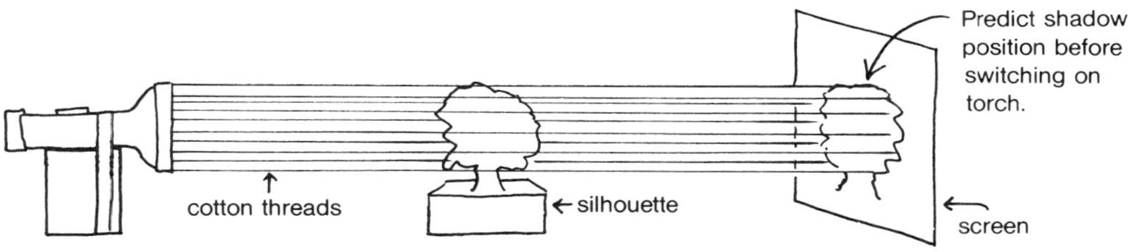

Area of study 25 | P of S 3c | LD 5

REFLECTION

C85

Purpose
To explain the basics of light reflection.

Materials needed
A slide projector and a slide card with a slit in it; a mirror, coloured filters.

Activity 1: Reflecting a light beam
Set up the slide projector with the slit card in place so that it shines a narrow beam of light just above a table. Advise the children of the proper use of the projector, for it can get hot. Let the children put a piece of paper on to the table, switch on the projector, and place the upended mirror in the path of the beam. If they swivel the mirror they will see that the light bounces off the mirror, but always at the same angle at which it struck the mirror.

Some of these angles can be drawn, using the light beam and mirror, on copymaster 85.

Activity 2: Effects of coloured filters
We see objects as coloured because the light 'bounced' off them to our eyes is red or blue or whichever other colours have been absorbed.

Using the same apparatus as in Activity 1, let the children look at the effects of shining the light beam through one or more filters. The filters absorb all but one colour, that of the resulting beam.

In daylight, the children can look through the filters and record what has happened to the colours of objects around the room.

Area of study 26 | P of S 3c | LD 5

MIRRORS

C86

Purpose
To find out about mirrors.

Materials needed
Single flat mirrors, pencil beam torches, mirrors taped together down one edge, concave and convex mirrors; a tall carton, plastic mirrors, greaseproof paper, beads, torch or lamp; a slide projector and a slide card with a slit in it.

Activity 1: Single mirror
Let the children take the initiative with a single mirror and see what they can find out about it. If they get stuck you will have to give them clues which may lead them to do some of the following things: draw half a picture and complete it with a reflected image; draw a picture with an axis of symmetry and put the mirror on the axis; play around with the mirror and pictures in books and comics, giving people two heads, etc; explore what

happens to the beam of light from a pencil torch when it is shone at the mirror.

Some of their discoveries can be recorded on copymaster 86.

Activity 2: Two mirrors
The children can see what happens when two mirrors are put together. With two mirrors taped together along a short side, as shown, they can explore the images produced.

Activity 3: Concave and convex mirrors
Let the children explore the images produced by these kinds of mirror and their uses.

Activity 4: Make a periscope
This way of making a periscope (and the kaleidoscope below) comes from Neil Ardley's 'My Science Book of Light'.

Show the children how to make a periscope, by fixing two plastic mirrors at the appropriate angles to one another within a carton or tall cardboard cuboid. You need an eye hole in the appropriate place to see one mirror, and an entry panel for light to reach the other mirror. These diagrams show how to make it.

Discuss with the children what is happening to enable us to see round corners, using reflected light.

Activity 5: Make a kaleidoscope
(Refer to the diagram below). Tape together three rectangular mirrors all of the same size, along their longer sides. Stick greaseproof or other translucent paper over one end of the resulting prism. Cut a 'lid' to fit the other and make a small hole in the centre before sticking it down. Drop beads through the hole, and then look into the prism through the hole, while allowing a small lamp or torch to shine on the translucent end. The 'repeat' pattern is the result of multiple reflection. Here are some diagrams showing how it is made.

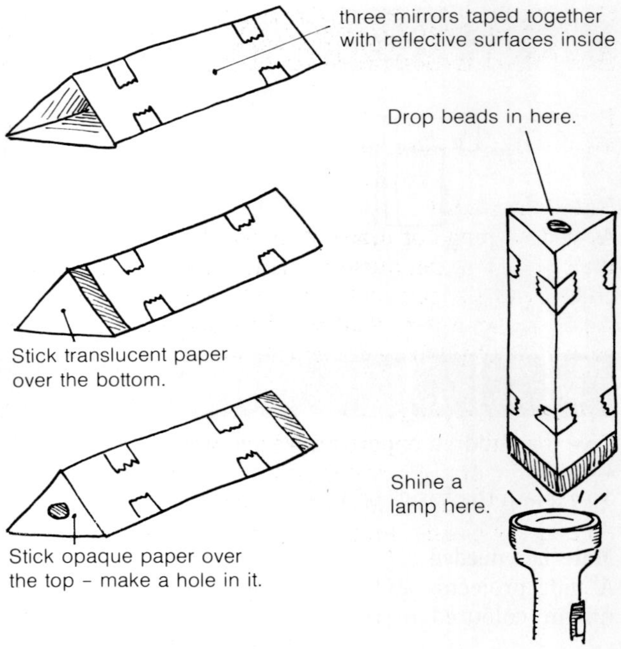

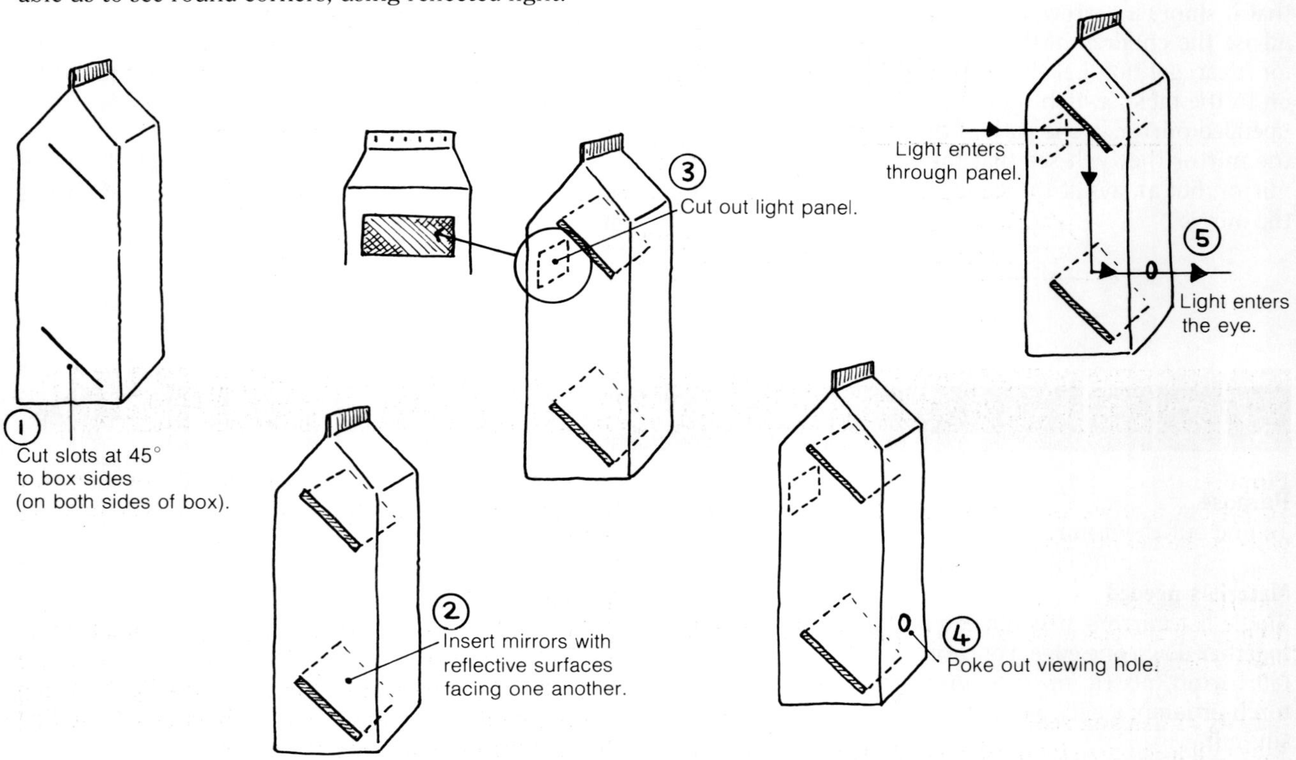

Programme of study: Physical processes

3. Light and sound

Pupils should be taught:

seeing

d that we see light sources, *e.g. light bulbs, candles,* because light from them enters our eyes.

Area of study 27 | P of S 3d | LD 4

LIGHT, COLOUR AND SHADE

Purpose
To draw light, colour and shade.

Materials needed
As wide a range of drawing materials and surfaces to draw on as you can muster, including pencils, charcoal, chalks, pastels, pens, felt tips and newsprint, cartridge paper, sugar paper, chalkboards; black and white and colour photographs; a camera and film.

Activity 1: Drawing
Give the children opportunities and time to experiment with all the drawing materials to depict light and shade in their pictures. When there are strong shadows in and around the classroom, point them out to the children, and let them have a good look at what happens to colours and shapes when they are in deep shadow.

Activity 2: Looking at photographs
Display a selection of photographs which show light and shade. Black and white pictures are particularly good because the colour does not distract the eye from the light and shade. The children could try representing the shadows they can see in these pictures using other drawing materials.

Activity 3: Taking photographs
You or the children can take photographs in and around the school, to show light and shade. Tell them that taking photographs is like drawing with the eye!

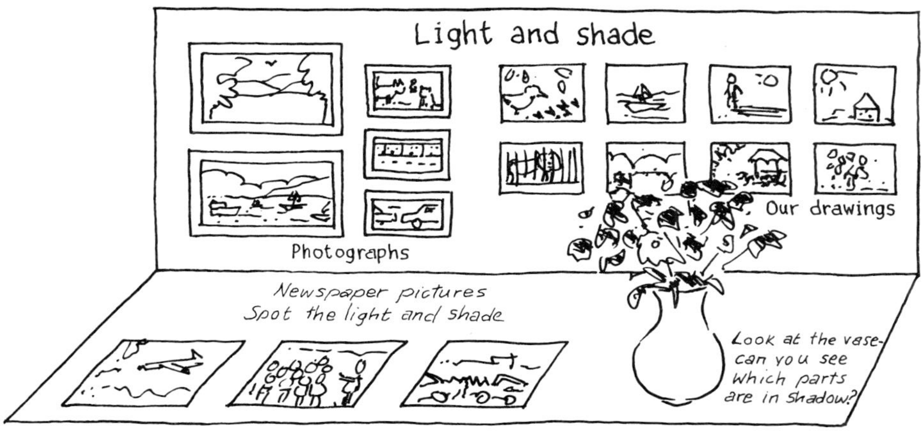

Area of study 28 | P of S 3d | LD 5

LOOKING

Purpose
To explain that we see things when light scattered off objects reaches our eyes.

Materials needed
A darkroom, stock cupboard or other completely dark place; colour filters.

Activity 1: Can you see?
Take children into a totally darkened room. They will be unable to see anything. Put on the light or open the curtains and they will see everything. We need light for sight.

Activity 2: Colour filters
If the children view their surroundings through these they will see that everything takes on the hue of the filter. Tell the children that this is because light is being 'bounced' off everything in many directions, including through the filter and into their eyes.

Programme of study: Physical processes

3. Light and sound

vibrations and sound

Pupils should be taught:

e that sounds are made when objects, *e.g. strings on musical instruments,* vibrate but that vibrations are not always directly visible;

f that the pitch and loudness of sounds produced by some vibrating objects, *e.g. a drum skin, a plucked string,* can be changed;

g that vibrations from sound sources can travel through a variety of materials, *e.g. metals, wood, glass, air,* to the ear.

Area of study 29 | P of S 3e, f | LD 2

MUSICAL INSTRUMENTS

C87

Purpose
To explain how musical sounds are produced in some musical instruments.

Materials needed
A collection of musical instruments, including at least one percussion, one wind and one stringed instrument; containers with fitting tops; dried pulses, rice and pasta to make shakers, jam jars, stout boxes, rubber bands, wooden blocks or rods, pieces of hard plastic and metal pipe, string.

Activity 1: Looking at instruments
Look at and discuss with the children the shape and construction of a range of instruments. Include at least one percussion (e.g. drum, piano), one wind (e.g. clarinet, recorder), and one stringed instrument (e.g. violin, guitar). Listen to them being played on tape. If possible ask a child or teacher who plays each of the instruments to come and tell the children about the different parts, how it works, and show them how it is played.

Activity 2: Shakers
Make shakers by putting dried pulses, rice or pasta into jars with well-fitting lids. Add them to the percussion instruments.

Activity 3: String things
A really stout cardboard or plastic box will support a rubber band or string stretched tightly around it. The 'string' does need to be very taut. The children can try plucking or scraping the 'string'. (See the diagram above.)

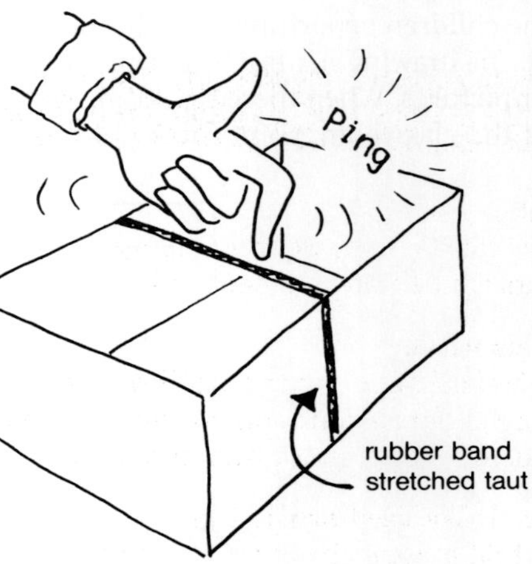

Activity 4: Things to bang
A row of jam jars with different amounts of coloured water in them sound melodic when tapped with a stick. Try tapping two wooden blocks together. Suspend pieces of wood, plastic pipe and metal pipe and try tapping those.

Create a music corner where the children can go and experiment quietly with a range of instruments and use junk materials to produce their own. (See the top of the next page for suggestions.) Display pictures of instruments from other cultures and try to borrow some if they are available.

Copymaster 87 can be used for the children's pictures of instruments.

Area of study 30 | P of S 3g | LD 2

EARS

Purpose
To show that we hear when sound reaches our ears, and that ears are delicate and need care.

Materials needed
Earmuffs; books and pictures of different animals, showing their ears; information about looking after our ears, and introductory books about what it means to be deaf.

Activity 1: We need ears to hear
Ask a child to wear the earmuffs and stand with his/her back to you, several paces away. Whisper a sentence. Get him/her to take off the earmuffs and repeat what they heard. It is unlikely they heard it all. Now get them to stand in the same position without the earmuffs, and whisper another sentence. They should hear it and be able to repeat it.

Activity 2: Outer ear shape and size
Explain that what we can see of our ears is the outer ear, and the part which does the work is inside our heads. Out outer ears collect sound, but are not terribly efficient, for they cannot move. Let the children name and find out about animals which have outer ears that they can move in the direction of the sound (e.g. cats, dogs and rabbits).

Activity 3: Care of ears
Discuss with the children that their ears are delicate instruments, that they should be kept clean but that they should NEVER put anything into their ears. Explain the dangers of repeated loud noise, of shouting down people's ears or smacking their ears.

Begin to discuss how deaf people communicate. Make sure the children understand that deaf people are just the same as hearing people, apart from in one respect, and they should not be treated as though they are silly.

Create a display of pictures of animal ears, ear care and 'sounds we like'.

Area of study 31 | P of S 3g | LD 4

SOUND TRAVELS THROUGH MATERIALS

Purpose
To show that sound travels through materials other than air.

Materials needed
A solid wooden door, a long piece of wood 54 cm × 10 cm and about 2 m long, pieces of soft cloth, rubber bands

and a clock with an audible tick; tin cans, a nail, a hammer, string and large beads; a kitchen roll tube; polystyrene tiles, or other material suitable for sound-proofing, craft glue and a large shoe box; a plastic bag, a see-through tank filled with water.

Activity 1: Sound travels through wood (1)
Ask a pair of children to stand either side of a door. If one child stands with his/her ear to the door, the other should be able to whisper a message through the door, if they have their lips close to it.

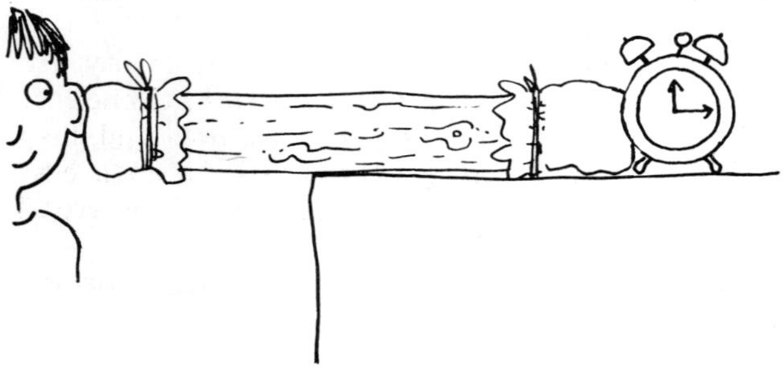

Activity 2: Sound travels through wood (2)
Tie pieces of soft cloth on to the ends of a long piece of wood. Let one child put one end of the cloth-clad wood to his/her ear. Place the clock so that it touches the other end of the wood. The tick can be heard through the wood.

Activity 3: Sound travels through string
Puncture the ends of two empty cans using the hammer and nail, and push the ends of a long piece of string through. Tie off the string with a bead at the end to prevent the knot pulling through. Two children can use this like a telephone, by pulling the string taut and whispering to one another. They can experiment to find out whether it works best with a string of any particular length.

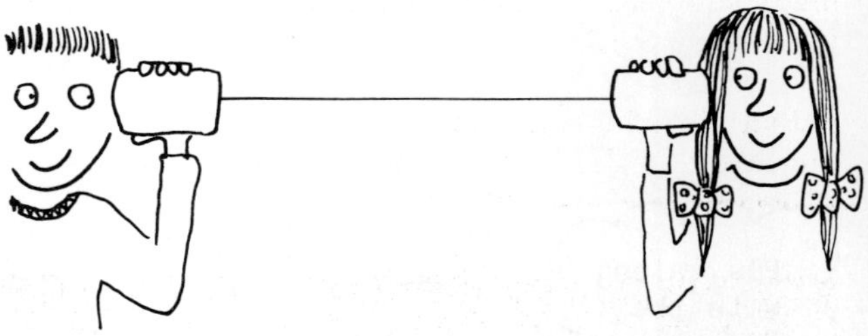

Activity 4: Sound travels through us!
Using a kitchen roll tube pressed gently against the chest, a little to the left of the middle, the children can listen to each other's heartbeat through the ribcage. If it proves too faint, ask the child whose heartbeat is to be heard to run up and down on the spot for a couple of minutes. Then listen.

Activity 5: Sound travels through water
Put a clock with a loud tick in a waterproof plastic bag. Lower the clock into a tank of water. The children should be able to hear the ticking by pressing their ears to the tank.

Activity 6: What does 'sound-proof' mean?
Explain to the children that when we want to keep out noise we can put a layer of something which is not very good at letting sound travel through it, all around a room. This is done in recording studios, and sometimes between the floors of blocks of flats. Try 'sound-proofing' a shoe box with polystyrene (take care: if cut with a heat cutter, polystyrene gives off toxic fumes) or cotton wadding. Put a clock with an audible tick into the box and close the lid. The tick should be noticeably quieter.

Area of study	P of S	LD
32	3g	4

REFLECTING SOUND

Purpose
To learn that sound can be reflected.

Materials needed
Paper, sticky tape, card, a clock or watch; books about bats and echo-sounding.

Activity 1: Listening for echoes
The school buildings may be placed so that you can stand between them and hear an echo when you shout. Alternatively, there may be a railway arch, subway or similar construction near the school where the children can hear echoes of their own voices. Explain to them that when we hear an echo, sound is 'bouncing back' to us, and the fact that the echo happens after we speak shows that sound takes time to travel.

Activity 2: Reflecting sound
Make two long cylinders from paper or thin card. Place them at angles to a large piece of stiff card held upright. Put a ticking clock or watch near one of the cylinders at the open end. Let a child put their ear to the other. The ticking will be heard quite clearly, for it has been reflected off the card.

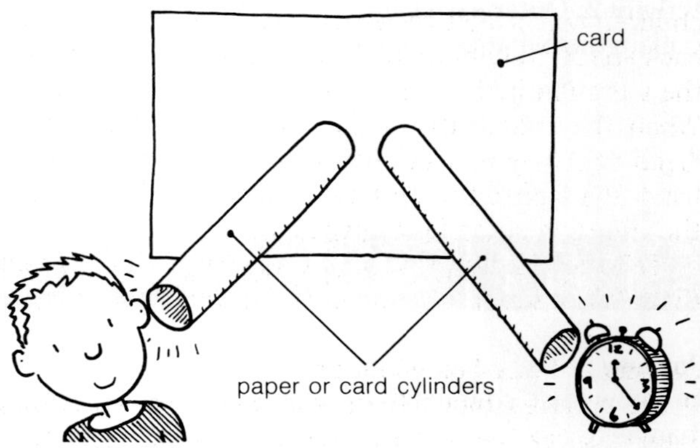

Activity 3: Bats and echoes
Let the children find out how bats manage to catch insect prey on the wing, in almost total darkness, without bumping into anything.

Activity 4: Echo-sounding
The search for shoals of fish, sunken boats or submarines, treasure and even the Loch Ness monster, involves sending sound waves to the river, lake or sea bed. Special equipment records the time taken for the echo to be received and thus the depth of water, and whether there is anything under the water surface or on the river, lake or sea bed.

Area of study 33 | P of S 3g | LD 4

SPEED OF LIGHT AND SOUND

C88

Purpose
To show that sound takes time to travel.

Materials needed
A cricket match, a drum.

Activity 1: Thunder and lightning
Remind the children that in a thunderstorm we can see the lightning before we hear the thunder, even though they are happening at the same time. The sound of the flash takes longer to reach us than the sight of it. In fact if you count in seconds between the flash and the first roll of thunder you can tell approximately how far away the thunder and lightning occurred; five seconds means it is one mile away.

Activity 2: Cricket and sound on the playing field
If the children watch a cricket game they will *see* the batsman strike the ball before they *hear* the sound of it. You can test out this observation if you have a long enough playing field at school. On a calm day, try standing a child with a drum and drumstick at one end. If the remaining children stand at the other end, they may just detect a time lag between seeing a single beat on the drum and hearing it. It takes about one second for sound to travel 330 m.

Let the children record this experiment in cartoon form on copymaster 88.

H 123=

Activity 3: Speed data
Tell the children that sound travels at about 1 070 feet per second (330 m per second) and light travels at 186 000 miles per second (that is 300 000 000 m per second). Compare this with other speed information like the fastest aircraft or land animals. Some aircraft travel faster than sound (that is through the sound barrier).

Area of study 34 | P of S 3e, f | LD 5

SOUND PRODUCTION

C89

Purpose
To show that vibrating things produce sounds.

Materials needed
A stringed instrument, a home-made rubber-band instrument; a tuning fork; string and fishing lines of various thicknesses, nails, hammer, balsa wood, weights; natural history books; a drum or tambour, sand, a tuning fork.

Activity 1: Vibration in instruments
If you pluck the strings on a violin or guitar, the children will be able to see the movement of the string back and forth (vibration). They may also be able to feel the vibration by touching the body of the instrument. When they pluck the rubber band on a home-made 'band box' they may be able to see the vibration of the band. If a tapped tuning fork is placed on the forehead the vibration of the fork can be felt.

Tell the children that vibration occurs in all things that make a sound.

Activity 2: Voice-box vibration
If the children touch their own voice-box when they hum or speak they can feel the vibration. Using natural history books let the children investigate the voices and the production of sounds by a range of animals.

Activity 3: Loudspeakers and vibration
If the school has a stereo sound system with speakers, the children can gently put their hand on the speaker when there is sound coming through, and feel the vibration.

Activity 4: Effects of string thickness
If you have a guitar available, the children can look at the thickness of the strings, and pluck and scrape each string in turn. They will notice that thicker strings produce lower notes. In addition to, or instead of a guitar, fix some strings and nylon fishing lines across a board or table, as shown at the top of the next page. Use a piece of balsa wood as a bridge in each case, and secure weights to the free end of the strings, adding weights until the string is really taut. The children can pluck and scrape the strings and note the link between thickness and whether the note produced is low or high.

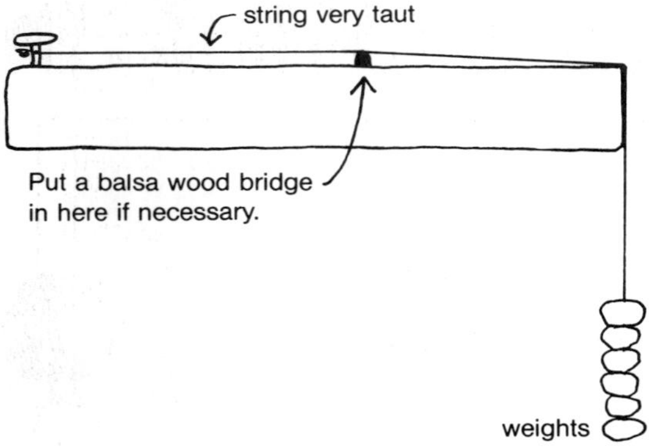

Activity 5: Sound makes things vibrate in a regular way
From their earlier activities the children will know that something vibrates to make sound. If you drop a little sand on the membrane of a tambour and stand a tuning fork that has been struck in the centre, the sand forms into concentric circles.

The children can record the results of this experiment pictorially on copymaster 89.

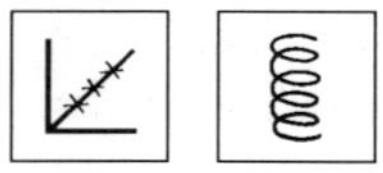

Area of study 35 | P of S 3f | LD 5

FREQUENCY, PITCH, AMPLITUDE

Purpose
To learn the meaning of frequency, pitch and amplitude.

Materials needed
Tuning forks of different pitch, an oscilloscope, microphone and tone generator.

Activity 1: Tuning forks
Let the children examine and strike the tuning forks. The forks may be marked with the note they make and the number of vibrations (often called cycles) per second. If they are unmarked tell the children that forks giving higher notes vibrate more quickly. For example:

middle C is 256 vibrations (cycles) per second
top C is 512 vibrations (cycles) per second.

Activity 2: A look at frequency
Borrow an oscilloscope from a secondary school and show the children what it does. They will be able to show, using their own voices, that frequency (as shown by the waves) changes according to how high or low the sound received is (i.e. its pitch).

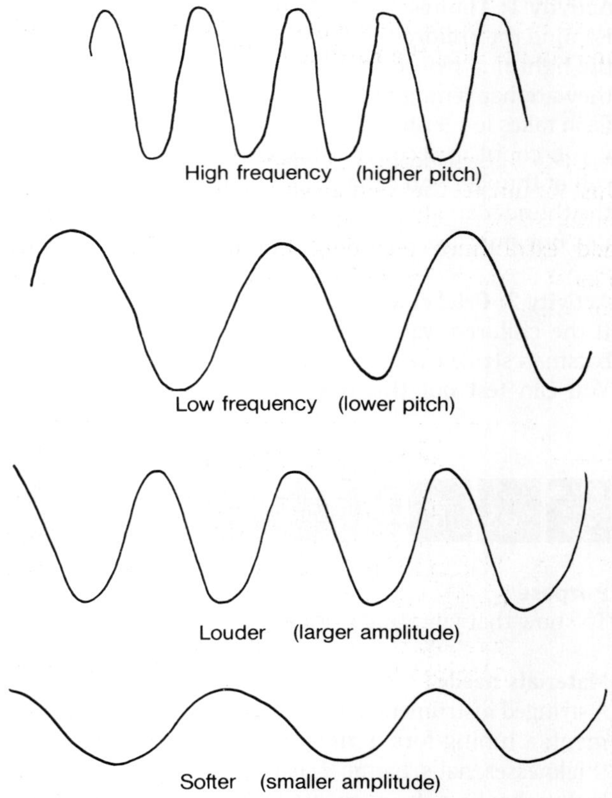

Activity 3: A look at amplitude
Set up an oscilloscope and the other apparatus. Let the children try singing a note or playing a note on an instrument softly and loudly. Observe what happens to the waves on the oscilloscope. The extent of the 'peak' and 'trough' of the wave should increase as the note gets louder. We call this *amplitude*.

Programme of study: Physical processes

4. The Earth and beyond Pupils should be taught:

the Sun, Earth and Moon **a** that the Sun, Earth and Moon are approximately spherical;

Area of study 36 | P of S 4a | LD 2

EARTH, SUN AND MOON

C90

Purpose
To learn that the Earth, Sun and Moon are separate spherical bodies.

Materials needed
Videos of weather forecasts, appropriate computer software, books and charts about the Earth, Sun and Moon; an orrery.

Activity 1: The Earth
Look at videos of weather forecasts showing satellite pictures of the Earth and computer software pictures of the Earth. Search books for photographs of the Earth taken from space. Have a good look at all the pictures and discuss what the Earth looks like.

Activity 2: Our location on planet Earth
Just for fun, let the children work out their own address, or the school address, taking it up to the postcode. Then add extra lines recording Country… UK, Europe, Planet… Earth, The universe. Address a giant envelope for display.

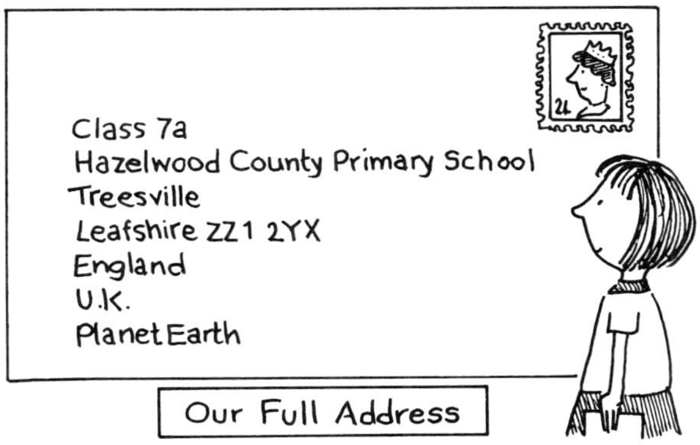

Activity 3: The Sun and Moon
Look at books and charts to find pictures of the Sun and Moon and talk about your findings. Details of American and Russian space trips will yield photographs of the Moon and its surface.

Borrow an orrery and show the children the relative positions, size and motions of the Earth, Sun and Moon.

Copymaster 90 is a worksheet on which the children can record some Earth, Sun and Moon facts. Tell the children that the outlines are not drawn to scale.

Programme of study: Physical processes

4. The Earth and beyond

periodic changes

Pupils should be taught:

b that the position of the Sun appears to change during the day, and how shadows change as this happens;

c that the Earth spins around its own axis, and how day and night are related to this spin;

d that the Earth orbits the Sun once each year, and that the Moon takes approximately 28 days to orbit the Earth.

Area of study 37 | P of S 4b | LD 4

THE SUN AND TIME OF DAY

C91–93

Purpose
To show that time used to be and can still be measured using the Sun, because its position in the sky appears to change during the day.

Materials needed
Sunshine! Protective eye gear for observing the Sun, chalk, a stick and a chair, stiff card, protractors and scissors.

Activity 1: The Sun's position and time of day
Set aside a period of time for doing this work, when the Sun shines. Get the children to observe and record the position of the Sun in the sky at 9.15 a.m., 11.30 a.m.,

1.30 p.m. and 3.15 p.m. (or at four other times which are better suited to your school timetable).

The children's record can be done on copymaster 91, or a class display can be made (see illustration at the bottom of the page).

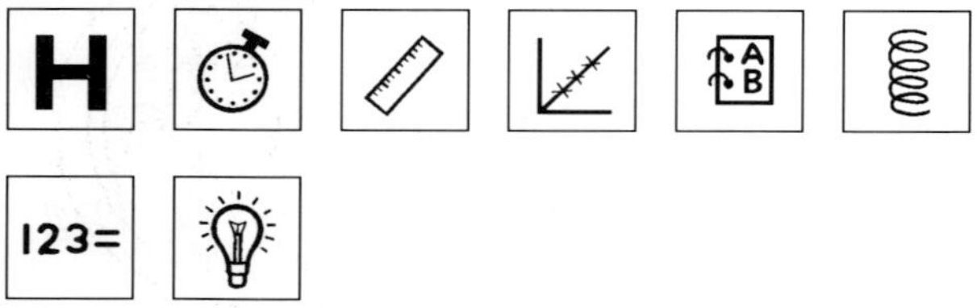

On the next sunny day the children may be able to estimate the time of day by consulting the Sun instead of a clock.

Activity 2: Shadow sticks

Push a stick, e.g. a broomstick, into the ground outside, away from buildings. Let the children mark and comment on the length and position of the stick's shadow at four times of day (say 9.30 a.m., 11.30 a.m., 1.30 p.m. and 3.30 p.m.). Let the children predict the length and position of the shadow in relation to the stick and draw it on paper. They can check their predictions by going and looking at the stick and its shadow. The next sunny day they can look first at the stick and its shadow and predict what the time is.

The children can do a similar investigation using a chair in the playground, or the shadow cast by the school building itself.

Activity 3: Sundials

Look at sundials. There may be one in a nearby garden. The local garden centre may bring some along for you to see, or the children may be allowed to visit the garden centre. The children need to draw a variety of designs and styles of sundials which will show them that sundials have been used across the ages. Rubbings can be made and the materials from which sundials are made can be studied.

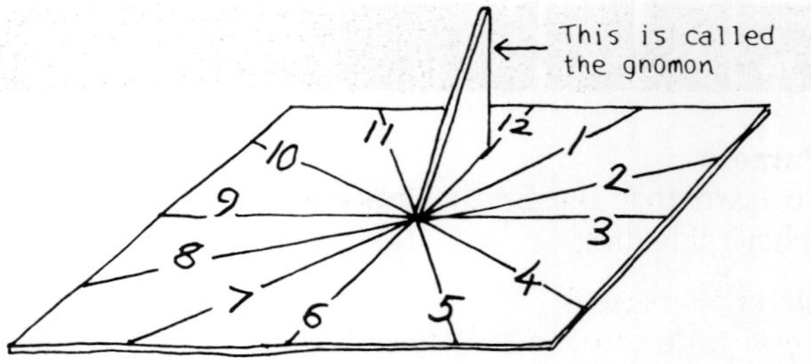

Give the children some stiff card and a protractor and scissors and ask them to create a sundial. They will need to create a pointer which is a right-angled triangle with an angle of inclination the same as the latitude of your location, and to calibrate the dial by 'setting' it in exactly the same position every time they take it out to use: i.e. with the long side of the triangle pointing towards the north.

The children can record what their own sundial looks like, in addition to some of the designs they have seen on other sundials, on copymaster 92.

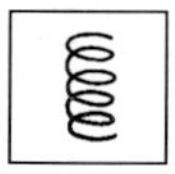

Activity 4: Telling the time by the Sun

On a day when you are sure the Sun is going to shine (!) remove or cover the clock and collect the children's watches. Give them to the headteacher for safe keeping. At a time that you have decided upon, say 11.10 a.m., ask the children to record what they think the exact time is by using their sundial.

When the children have completed their recording on copymaster 93 tell them what the exact time was.

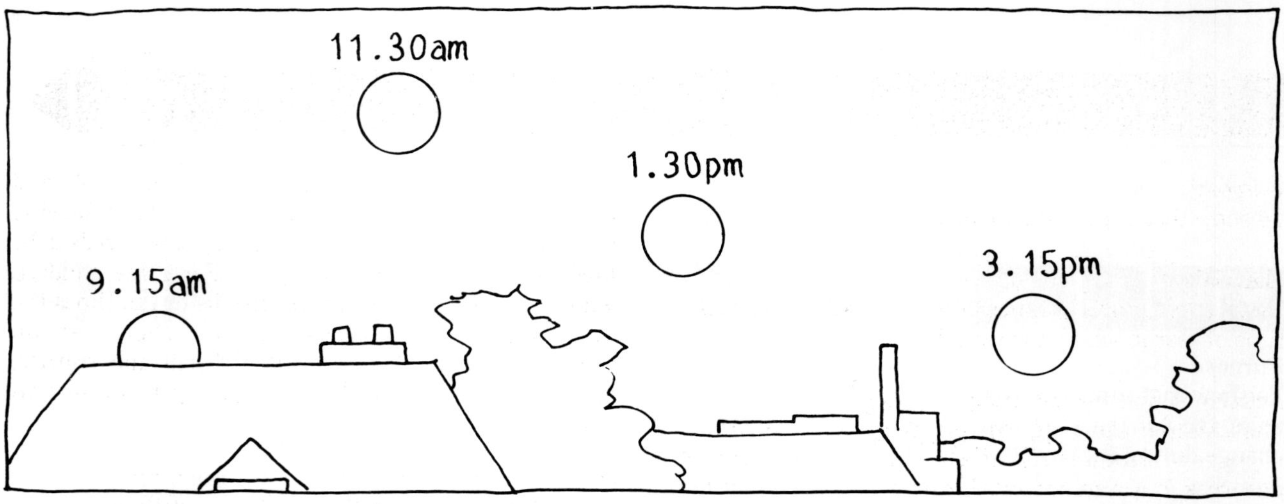

Class display: The Sun's position and time of day

Area of study 38 | P of S 4c | LD 5

WHY NIGHT OCCURS

Purpose
To explain why we have night-time.

Materials needed
Powerful torch, lampshade with orange cloth or tissue to cover, classroom globe; card sheets and string to make sandwich-boards, a map of the world (to copy), felt tips.

Activity 1: Day and night
Discuss with the children what daylight is and what night is. They may be able to say that our light comes from the Sun, that when there is no sunlight we are in darkness and this is what we call night. The problem then is to show why the Sun does not always give us light.

Explain that the reason we have day and night is that the world spins on its axis while the Sun remains still. Darken the room. Place a lit torch inside a covered lampshade to represent the Sun. Use a classroom globe or a balloon to represent the Earth and, holding it some short distance away from, but on a level with the 'Sun', turn it on a north-south axis. The children can then see that part of the 'Earth' is lit by the 'Sun' while part remains in darkness. As the 'Earth' moves on its axis, the part that was in darkness moves into the light, while the part that was formerly light moves into darkness.

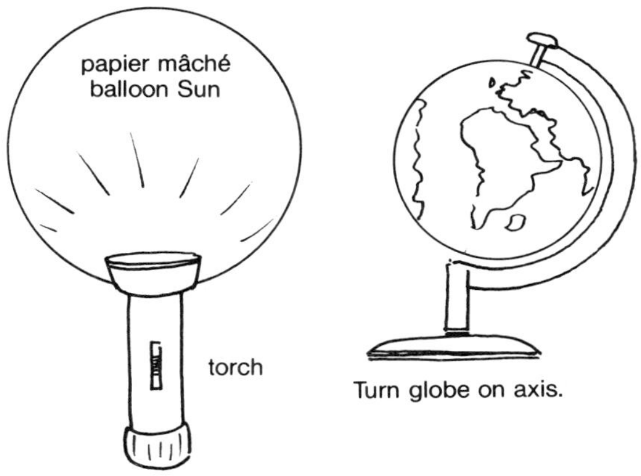

Activity 2: The rotating Earth
Make four placards or sandwich-boards which children can wear on their backs. Draw a quarter of the world map on each one so that together they form a flat picture of the world (see illustration below). Make one plain orange sandwich-board to represent the Sun, and get the child wearing this to hold a lamp or torch. If the children wearing the world sandwich-boards stand in a circle close together and link hands or arms, they can walk round in a circle to represent the turning of the Earth on its axis. The 'Sun' child can shine the torch on the moving Earth and the children will see that only part of the Earth gets the Sun's light at any one time.

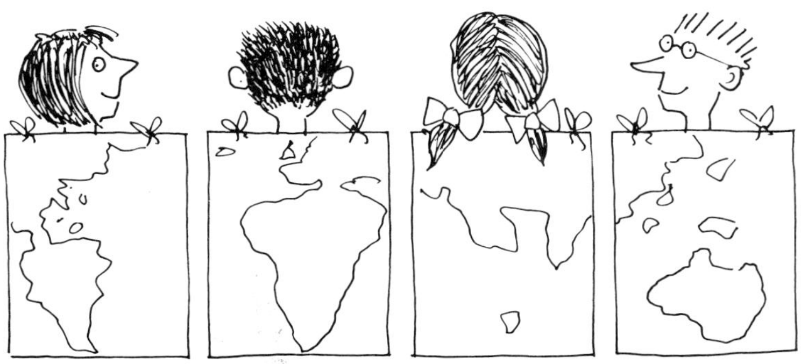

Area of study 39 | P of S 4c | LD 5

LENGTH OF DAY

C94

Purpose
To show that day length changes throughout the year.

Materials
Newspaper reports of times of sunrise and sunset at the time of year in which the work is done.

Activity 1: Sunrise and sunset
The children can note whether they had breakfast in daylight or darkness and at what time that was during one week in November and during one week in July. On those same days they could note the time the lights went on in their home in the evening.

The children's knowledge about nightfall and daylight can be recorded on copymaster 94. Following their winter-time recording, the copymaster needs to be filed for use in the summer term. For those children who are unable to record these details or the times the Sun came up and went down, you can show them on their copymaster the times of nightfall and sunrise, using the times recorded in the newspaper as your own resource.

Area of study 40 | P of S 4d | LD 5

THE SUN AND OUR YEAR

C95

Purpose
To find out that the Sun's inclination in the sky changes from one part of the year to another.

Materials needed
Protective eyeshade for viewing the Sun. (Ask the school doctor what is suitable to shield the eyes from the Sun. Do not use sun-glasses. The exposed ends of a developed roll of photographic film may be appropriate.) Prepared display board with stick-on Sun, or pen for drawing on the window.

Activity 1: Sun's position in the sky
Twice in the school year, perhaps around the longest and shortest days (June and December) set aside a week or so in which this experiment can be done. On the first sunny day in each of these periods, get each child in turn to don protective eye gear and observe the position of the Sun in the sky at 11.30 a.m. or thereabouts. If the Sun shines directly into the classroom, its position can be marked on a strategic window. If not, prepare a display board with the view of the skyline from the school, and the children can transfer their observations as stick-on Suns on the board. A comparison of the results at both times of year should show that the Sun is higher in the sky at 11.30 a.m. in the summer than it is in the winter.

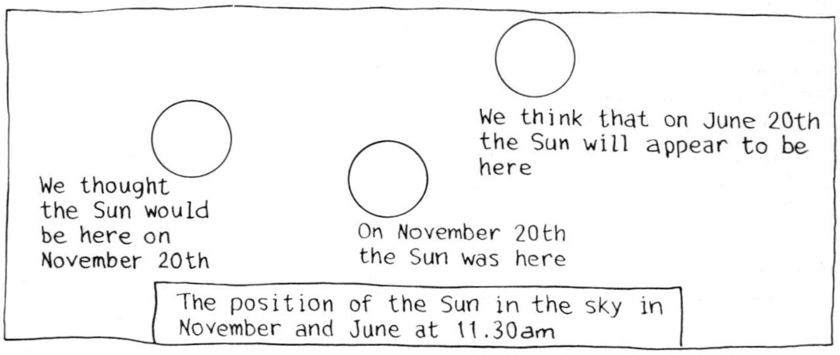

Activity 2: Shadows
For two periods in the year, which may be one week or two depending on the weather pattern in your area, watch out for the first sunny day. Then at a time you have pre-set to fit your timetable (but somewhere around the middle of the day) get the children to go into the playground in pairs. On a spot they can remember and identify, ask them to draw around each other's shadow. They can measure and record the 'heights' of their shadows. Experimental results should show that the shadows are shorter in the summer months when the Sun is higher in the sky. To fully understand this work the children need to have mastered Area of study 24, *Light travels in straight lines*, page 90.

The children can record their results on copymaster 95.

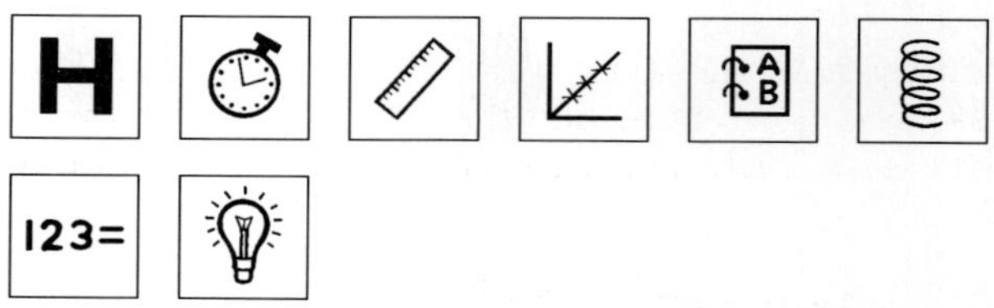

If a classroom display is mounted, several Suns can be placed on the board at different heights in the sky. If a thread is then pinned taut from each Sun over the little figure set on the ground, the children can see how the length of the 'shadow' behind the figure varies with the inclination of the Sun.

Area of study 41 | P of S 4d | LD 5

MOON PHASES

C96

Purpose
To observe and record the shape changes the Moon appears to undergo throughout the month.

Materials needed
Clear skies. Books about the Moon, paper and card, a projector and screen and a ball, an orrery.

Activity 1: The Moon's appearance
This work is best done in the second half of the autumn term. When the clocks go back, nightfall occurs before the children's bedtime, but after school has finished. Before you start this work you will need to ask parents if their children may do this work at home. You can say that it will only involve a few minutes once a week. When you have parental permission, then ask the children to look at the night sky on the next Monday night.

If they can see the Moon they can record its shape on their record sheet, copymaster 96. If they cannot see the Moon, then they should look out every evening that week until they spot it. Then the following week they should do the same and draw what they see. When they have made a drawing (if possible) in each of four consecutive weeks, they can bring their work back to school for discussion.

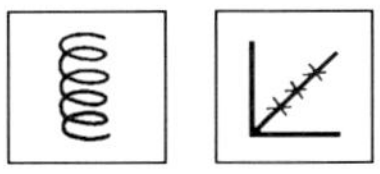

Activity 2: Moon facts
Ask the children to consult the reference sources about the Moon. Each new discovery can be recorded on a strip of paper and the children can then collate the facts under headings they devise themselves. In fact, with a little help from you they can create their own display.

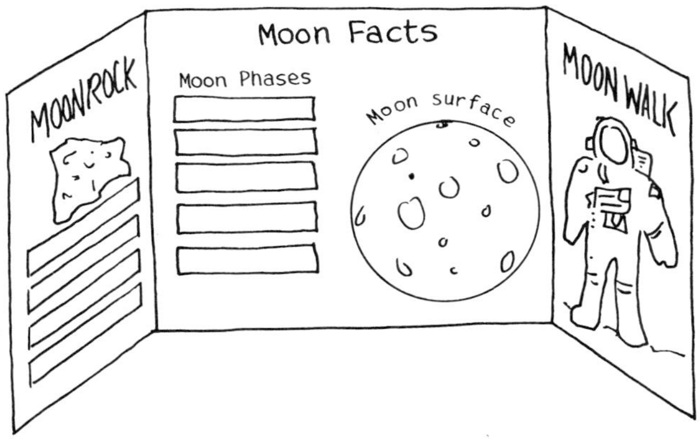

Activity 3: Moon simulation
Take a small piece of card and trim it to fit a slide frame. Poke a pencil through the card to produce a circular hole. Use a slide projector to project a circular pool of light. Darken the room. Then if you pass a ball through the light it will appear to change shape just as the Moon does in its phases (see the diagram below).

Activity 4: Eclipses of the Moon
Explain to the children that an eclipse of the Moon happens when the Earth passes between the Moon and the Sun so that the Moon's orbit is in the Earth's shadow. Show the children how this can happen using an orrery.

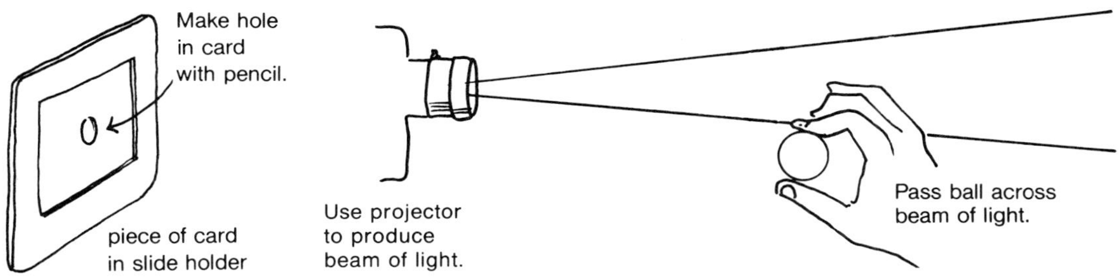

Area of study 42 | P of S 4d | LD 5

OUR EARTH IN RELATION TO THE SUN

C97

Purpose
To revise and extend a knowledge of the movement of the Earth about the Sun.

Materials needed
A globe and a torch, reference books about the planets, especially the Earth, information about time zones.

Activity 1: Earth year
The experiment which showed day and night (Area of Study 38 *Why night occurs,* page 101) can be repeated, and this time as well as rotating the globe on its axis it can be moved around the Sun to demonstrate the time we call a year.

Activity 2: Time zones

Because of the rotation of the Earth the time is different in different parts of the world. Some major banks and large hotels have clocks showing times around the world. If it is not possible to show these to the children you can arrange an array of clocks in the classroom to show time in different time zones across the world. You will need to find out where the time zones fall.

The children can decide on a moment when they are going to record time across the world on copymaster 97.

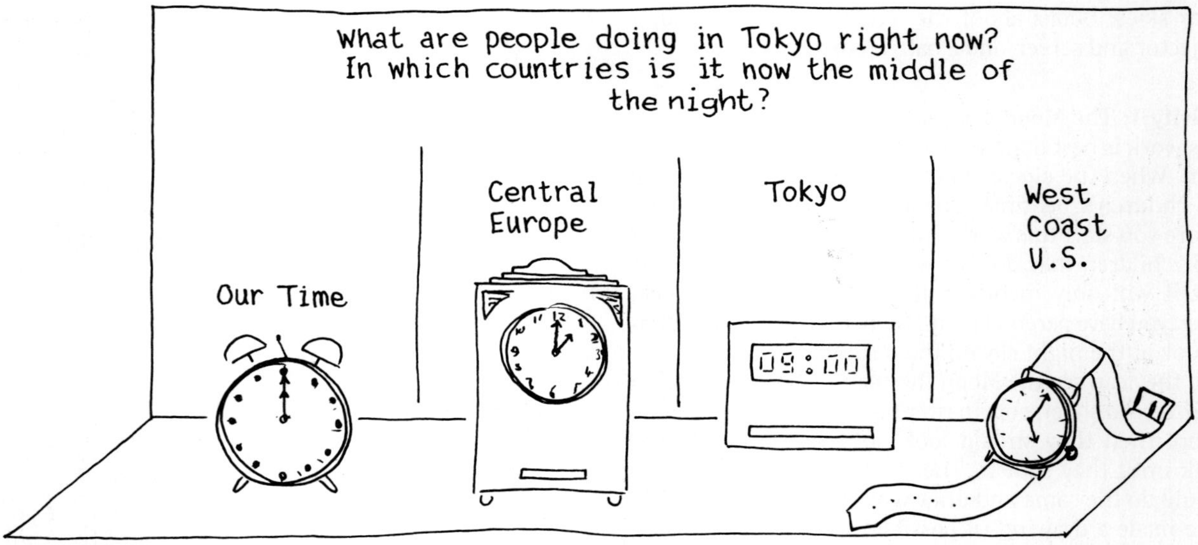

RECORD SHEETS 1–2

Experimental and investigative science

RECORD SHEET 1

Key Stage Two

Name ____________________ **Year/Class** ____________________

Level			
Level 2			
		123=	
Level 3			
	H		
		123=	
Level 4	H		
	SCIENCE	123=	
Level 5	H		
	DE		
			123=
	SCIENCE		

Life processes and living things, Materials and their properties, Physical processes

RECORD SHEET 2

Key Stage Two

Name ______________ **Year/Class** ______________

	Life processes and living things	Materials and their properties	Physical processes
Level 2 Comments			
Level 3 Comments			
Level 4 Comments			
Level 5 Comments			